David Bejou
Timothy L. Keiningham
Lerzan Aksoy
Editors

Customer Lifetime Value: Reshaping the Way We Manage to Maximize Profits

Customer Lifetime Value: Reshaping the Way We Manage to Maximize Profits has been co-published simultaneously as *Journal of Relationship Marketing*, Volume 5, Numbers 2/3 2006.

Pre-publication REVIEWS, COMMENTARIES, EVALUATIONS . . .

"**V**ERY APT AND USEFUL to academicians and practitioners who are struggling with this issue. . . . Does a wonderful job in demonstrating how to compute, measure, and manage customer lifetime value from different perspectives. . . . Focuses on viewing customers as assets and discusses issues and challenges for achieving customer lifetime value goals."

Jaideep Motwani, PhD
Chair and Professor of Management, Grand Valley State University Michigan

Best Business Books®
An Imprint of The Haworth Press, Inc.

Customer Lifetime Value: Reshaping the Way We Manage to Maximize Profits

Customer Lifetime Value: Reshaping the Way We Manage to Maximize Profits has been co-published simultaneously as *Journal of Relationship Marketing*, Volume 5, Numbers 2/3 2006.

Customer Lifetime Value: Reshaping the Way We Manage to Maximize Profits, edited by David Bejou, PhD, Timothy L. Keiningham, MBA, and Lerzan Aksoy, PhD (Vol. 5, No. 2/3, 2006). *Leading experts show how to leverage customer lifetime values (CLV) in all aspects of business, including customer management, employee management, and firm valuation.*

Capturing Customer Equity: Moving from Products to Customers, edited by David Bejou, PhD, and Gopalkrishnan R. Iyer, PhD (Vol. 5, No. 1, 2006). *An international collection of thought-provoking writing addressing important issues in the management of customer equity.*

The Future of Relationship Marketing, edited by David Bejou, PhD, and Adrian Palmer, PhD (Vol. 4, No. 3/4, 2005). *"If you are interested in relationship marketing THIS IS THE BOOK FOR YOU." (David T. Wilson, PhD, MBA, Clemens Professor of Marketing, Emeritus, Pennsylvania State University)*

Internal Relationship Management: Linking Human Resources to Marketing Performance, edited by Michael D. Hartline, PhD, and David Bejou, PhD (Vol. 3, No. 2/3, 2004). *"FINALLY, there is a scholarly book on internal employee relationship management. . . . Links human resources to marketing performance." (Jagdish N. Sheth, PhD, Charles H. Kellstadt Professor of Marketing, Emory University)*

Customer Relationship Management in Electronic Markets, edited by Gopalkrishnan R. Iyer, PhD, and David Bejou, PhD (Vol. 2, No. 3/4, 2003). *"Extremely helpful for business people and university faculty. I RECOMMEND THIS BOOK HIGHLY." (James E. Littlefield, PhD, Professor of Marketing, Virginia Polytechnic Institute and State University, Blacksburg)*

Customer Lifetime Value: Reshaping the Way We Manage to Maximize Profits

David Bejou, PhD
Timothy L. Keiningham, MBA
Lerzan Aksoy, PhD
Editors

Customer Lifetime Value: Reshaping the Way We Manage to Maximize Profits has been co-published simultaneously as *Journal of Relationship Marketing*, Volume 5, Numbers 2/3 2006.

Best Business Books®
An Imprint of The Haworth Press, Inc.

New York • London • Victoria (AU)
www.HaworthPress.com

Published by

Best Business Books®, 10 Alice Street, Binghamton, NY 13904-1580 USA

Best Business Books® is an imprint of The Haworth Press, Inc., 10 Alice Street, Binghamton, NY 13904-1580 USA.

Customer Lifetime Value: Reshaping the Way We Manage to Maximize Profits has been co-published simultaneously as *Journal of Relationship Marketing*, Volume 5, Numbers 2/3 2006.

The development, preparation, and publication of this work has been undertaken with great care. However, the publisher, employees, editors, and agents of The Haworth Press and all imprints of The Haworth Press, Inc., including The Haworth Medical Press® and The Pharmaceutical Products Press®, are not responsible for any errors contained herein or for consequences that may ensue from use of materials or information contained in this work. With regard to case studies, identities and circumstances of individuals discussed herein have been changed to protect confidentiality. Any resemblance to actual persons, living or dead, is entirely coincidental.

The Haworth Press is committed to the dissemination of ideas and information according to the highest standards of intellectual freedom and the free exchange of ideas. Statements made and opinions expressed in this publication do not necessarily reflect the views of the Publisher, Directors, management, or staff of The Haworth Press, Inc., or an endorsement by them.

Library of Congress Cataloging-in-Publication Data

Customer lifetime value : reshaping the way we manage to maximize profits / David Bejou, Timothy L. Keiningham, Lerzan Aksoy, editors.
    p. cm.
    Co-published simultaneously as Journal of Relationship Marketing, Volume 5, Numbers 2/3 2006.
    Includes bibliographical references and index.
    ISBN-13: 978-0-7890-3435-9 (hard cover : alk. paper)
    ISBN-10: 0-7890-3435-2 (hard cover : alk. paper)
    ISBN-13: 978-0-7890-3436-6 (soft cover : alk. paper)
    ISBN-10: 0-7890-3436-0 (soft cover : alk. paper)
    1. Relationship marketing. 2. Customer relations–Management. I. Bejou, David. II. Keiningham, Timothy L. III. Aksoy, Lerzan. Journal of relationship marketing (Binghamton, N.Y.)

HF5415.55.C874 2006
658.8'12–dc22

2006017120

Indexing, Abstracting & Website/Internet Coverage

This section provides you with a list of major indexing & abstracting services and other tools for bibliographic access. That is to say, each service began covering this periodical during the year noted in the right column. Most Websites which are listed below have indicated that they will either post, disseminate, compile, archive, cite or alert their own Website users with research-based content from this work. (This list is as current as the copyright date of this publication.)

(continued)

(continued)

Special Bibliographic Notes related to special journal issues (separates) and indexing/abstracting:

- indexing/abstracting services in this list will also cover material in any "separate" that is co-published simultaneously with Haworth's special thematic journal issue or DocuSerial. Indexing/abstracting usually covers material at the article/chapter level.
- monographic co-editions are intended for either non-subscribers or libraries which intend to purchase a second copy for their circulating collections.
- monographic co-editions are reported to all jobbers/wholesalers/approval plans. The source journal is listed as the "series" to assist the prevention of duplicate purchasing in the same manner utilized for books-in-series.
- to facilitate user/access services all indexing/abstracting services are encouraged to utilize the co-indexing entry note indicated at the bottom of the first page of each article/chapter/contribution.
- this is intended to assist a library user of any reference tool (whether print, electronic, online, or CD-ROM) to locate the monographic version if the library has purchased this version but not a subscription to the source journal.
- individual articles/chapters in any Haworth publication are also available through the Haworth Document Delivery Service (HDDS).

Customer Lifetime Value: Reshaping the Way We Manage to Maximize Profits

CONTENTS

ABOUT THE EDITORS

David Bejou, PhD, is Professor of Marketing and Dean of School of Business at Virginia State University. He previously served on the faculty of the University of North Carolina at Wilmington, where he was nominated in 1996 for the Chancellor Teaching Excellence Award, and nominated in both 1995 and 1996 for the Faculty Scholarship Award. He has also been a faculty member at several other universities in the United States and Australia.

Dr. Bejou has published widely in professional journals, including the *Journal of Services Marketing*, the *Journal of Business Research*, the *Journal of Marketing Management*, the *International Journal of Bank Marketing*, and the *European Journal of Marketing*. He is a member of the American Marketing Association and the Academy of Marketing Science, and has been a presenter or Session Chair at many national and international conferences.

Dr. Bejou has served as a marketing/promotions consultant to the United Carolina Bank (UCB), Brunswick Community College, and other businesses and community organizations.

Timothy L. Keiningham, MBA, is Senior Vice President and Head of Consulting at Ipsos Loyalty. He is author of several management books and numerous scientific papers. His most recent book, *Loyalty Myths* (with Vavra, Aksoy, and Wallard), 2005 by John Wiley and Sons, poses the fallacies of most of the conventional wisdom surrounding customer loyalty. He has received best paper awards from the *Journal of Marketing* and the *Journal of Service Research,* and has received the Citations of Excellence "Top 50" award (top 50 management papers of approximately 20,000 papers reviewed) for 2005 from Emerald Management Reviews. Another paper that he coauthored was a finalist for best paper in *Managing Service Quality*. Tim also received the 2006 best reviewer award from the *Journal of Service Research*. His articles have appeared in such publications as *Journal of Marketing, Journal of Service Re-*

search, Journal of Relationship Marketing, Interfaces, Marketing Management, Managing Service Quality, and *Journal of Retail Banking.* He serves on the editorial review board of *Journal of Marketing,* and the *Journal of Service Research,* and the advisory board of *Journal of Relationship Marketing.*

Lerzan Aksoy, PhD, is Assistant Professor of Marketing at Koç University in Istanbul, Turkey. She is co-author of the book *Loyalty Myths* (with Keiningham, Vavra, and Wallard), 2005 by John Wiley and Sons. Her article "The Brand-Customer Connection," (with Timothy L. Keiningham, Tiffany Perkins-Munn and Terry G. Vavra) was selected by Emerald Management Reviews as one of the top 50 management articles of 2005, from among 20,000 articles reviewed by that organization in that year. Her article "Should Recommendation Agents Think Like People" was a finalist for best paper in the *Journal of Service Research.* Her article, "Does Customer Satisfaction Lead to Profitability? The Mediating Role of Share-of-Wallet," was a finalist for best paper in *Managing Service Quality.* Her articles have been accepted for publication in such journals as *Journal of Marketing, Journal of Service Research, Journal of Relationship Marketing, International Journal of Service Industry Management, Managing Service Quality,* and *Marketing Management.* She serves on the advisory board of the *Journal of Relationship Marketing,* the editorial review board of *International Journal of Service Industry Management* and is an ad hoc reviewer for *Journal of Marketing, Journal of Service Research,* and *Cornell HRA Quarterly.*

How Customer Lifetime Value Is Changing How Business Is Managed

Timothy L. Keiningham

Ipsos Loyalty

Lerzan Aksoy

Koc University, Istanbul, Turkey

David Bejou

Virginia State University

SUMMARY. In the quest for sustainable competitive advantage, managers have sought to differentiate themselves through a customer (as opposed to product) focus. This has given rise to successive strategies designed to improve the customer experience (e.g., objective quality, service quality, customer satisfaction, customer retention, customer loyalty, etc.). The problem, however, is that a satisfied, loyal customer who is persuaded to consistently buy a firm's product or service over and over again because of its quality can be and often is unprofitable.

Timothy L. Keiningham, MBA, is Senior Vice President and Head of Consulting, Ipsos Loyalty, Morris Corporation Center 2, 1 Upper Pond Road, Building D, Parsippany, NJ 07054 (E-mail: tim.keiningham@ipsos-na.com).

Lerzan Aksoy, PhD, is Assistant Professor of Marketing, Koc University, College of Administrative Sciences and Economics, Rumeli Feneri Yolu, Sariyer 80910 Istanbul, Turkey (E-mail: laksoy@ku.edu.tr).

David Bejou, PhD, is Dean, School of Business, Virginia State University, P.O. Box 9398, Petersburg, VA 23806 (E-mail: dbejou@vsu.edu).

[Haworth co-indexing entry note]: "How Customer Lifetime Value Is Changing How Business Is Managed." Keiningham, Timothy L., Lerzan Aksoy, and David Bejou. Co-published simultaneously in *Journal of Relationship Marketing* (Best Business Books, an imprint of The Haworth Press, Inc.) Vol. 5, No. 2/3, 2006, pp. 1-6; and: *Customer Lifetime Value: Reshaping the Way We Manage to Maximize Profits* (ed: David Bejou, Timothy L. Keiningham, and Lerzan Aksoy) Best Business Books, an imprint of The Haworth Press, Inc., 2006, pp. 1-6. Single or multiple copies of this article are available for a fee from The Haworth Document Delivery Service [1-800-HAWORTH, 9:00 a.m. - 5:00 p.m. (EST). E-mail address: docdelivery@haworthpress.com].

Therefore, using such strategies does not guarantee increased profits. As a result, firms will increasingly rely on the measurement and management of customers' lifetime values to guide their customer loyalty efforts. doi:10.1300/J366v05n02_01 *[Article copies available for a fee from The Haworth Document Delivery Service: 1-800-HAWORTH. E-mail address: <docdelivery@haworthpress.com> Website: <http://www.HaworthPress.com>* © 2006 by The Haworth Press, Inc. All rights reserved.]

KEYWORDS. Customer lifetime value, strategic management, objectives, financial performance

The saga of business centers on a never-ending quest for the ultimate source of competitive advantage expected to lead to growth and profitability. In the intense competition of the late twentieth and early twenty-first century, many of the stalwarts of global enterprise competed largely by being more efficient than their competitors. Superior efficiency, however, has proven difficult to sustain . . . all too quickly becoming parity among competitors and a minimally acceptable expectation of consumers.

With heightened competition, parity is achieved at an ever-increasing rate. As a result, however, the modern era has seen mounting numbers of industry leaders stumble: even fail. In response, a host of pundits, prophets and snake-oil salesmen have put forth a multitude of paradigms aimed at steering companies away from the road to perdition toward the yellow-brick road to profitability.

At the core of most of these promises has been the call to adopt an external focus on customers (as opposed to an internal focus on production). Perhaps beginning in 1960, with Theodore Levitt's widely-quoted and reprinted *Harvard Business Review* article, "Marketing Myopia" (Levitt, 1960), customer focus has become widely regarded as "the" most sacred commandment of business management. If we examine the historical implementation of customer focus over the last forty years, however, we see an interesting pattern of evolution: one of successive mythologies.

The 1980s can be thought of as predominantly the decade of quality. Based on the impressive development of Japanese manufacturers, "Total Quality" and "Zero Defects" became the mantra of managers the world over. Quality, it was argued, paid for itself (e.g., *Quality is Free*: Crosby, 1979) by reducing rework and allowing firms to get closer to their customers.

Unfortunately, manufacturers found that objective quality was relatively easy for competitors to achieve. The result: objective quality wasn't paying the promised dividends. *Business Week* ran a cover story in 1994 lamenting the problem, with the cover emblazoned, "Making Quality Pay" (Greising, 1994). A 2005 *Wall Street Journal* article entitled "Rethinking Quality" shows that a decade hasn't changed the problem (White, 2005).

Following suit, services were quick to adopt the call for quality (for example, see Edvardsson, 1988; Parasuraman, Zeithaml, & Berry, 1985). Researchers proposed models for making service quality pay, and managers eagerly embraced them. In the spirit of the time, Mary Colby, Associate Editor, *Bank Marketing* magazine observed, "Service quality is shaping up as the marketing imperative of the '90s'" (Colby, 1992).

The subtle difference for service marketers was that the focus in services was on a customer's "perceived" quality as opposed to a product's "objective" quality (conformance to manufacturing specifications) of their manufacturing brethren. This resulted in a new mantra of "Customer Satisfaction." The quest for "100% satisfaction," became a strategic imperative. Consequently, the popularity of customer satisfaction programs soared rapidly.

The phrase "YOUR SATISFACTION IS GUARANTEED" became ubiquitous to the point of cliché. Whether it be expensive office equipment, a hotel stay, or a bag of cheese puffs, you could be certain that "your total satisfaction is guaranteed, or your money back" (Keiningham & Vavra, 2001). The conventional wisdom of the time was customer satisfaction brought profits.

Unfortunately, the fate of the customer satisfaction did not fare much better than the objective quality movement. In fact, the failure of countless customer satisfaction initiatives to demonstrate measurable returns caused many to openly challenge the value of such efforts (for example, see Council on Financial Competition, 1987). Some labeled satisfaction a "trap" (Reichheld, 1996); others declared it dead (Williams & Visser, 2002). Book titles such as *Customer Satisfaction Is Worthless* (Gitomer, 1998) and *Beyond Customer Satisfaction* (Bhote, 1996) reflected the disillusionment many managers had with customer satisfaction as a means for optimizing profitability.

Into the void, a superceding paradigm emerged: customer retention. Led by the seminal *Harvard Business Review* article, "Zero Defections: Quality Comes to Services" (Reichheld & Sasser, 1990), the 1990s can be reasonably thought of as the decade of customer loyalty. Improved retention rates were promised to result in remarkable financial returns.

The article went on to extol the virtues of minimizing customer attrition. "Customer defections have a surprisingly powerful impact on the bottom line. They can have more to do with a service company's profits than scale, market share, unit costs, and many other factors usually associated with competitive advantage. . . . Low-defection strategies can overwhelm low-cost strategies."

Business leaders around the world embraced this message. A worldwide survey of CEOs conducted by the Conference Board in 2002 found that customer loyalty and retention *was the most important challenge* that the CEOs believed they faced–more important than improving stock performance, reducing costs, or developing leaders within their organizations (Conference Board, 2002). As a result, firms spent billions of dollars in efforts to improve customer loyalty.

Unfortunately, as with the quality and satisfaction movements, the realized profits from improved customer loyalty haven't lived up to the hype. Expensive customer relationship management systems, considered by many to be integral to managing customer loyalty, frequently show themselves to be expensive boondoggles (Hughes, 2002; Patton, 2001). Similarly, loyalty rewards programs have reached omnipresence. Now even some of their most ardent supporters concede that their ability to impact customer attraction and retention is unsustainable at best (Colloquy, 2005) and the cost of these systems almost guarantees a negative return on investment (Cigiliano, Georgiadis, Pleasance, & Whalley, 2000). Not surprisingly, cries are arising proclaiming that many of the claims associated with loyalty are bunk (Reinartz & Kumar, 2002; Keiningham, Vavra, Aksoy, & Wallard, 2005).

Rising from the ashes, a new buzzword is creeping into the management lexicon designed to supercede customer loyalty–customer experience management (for example, Conference Board, 2006; Gordon, 2005; Pine & Gilmore, 1998; Schmitt, 2003). In their book *The Future of Competiton*, Prahalad and Ramaswamy (2004, p. 137) argue that "value is now centered in the experiences of customers" and not just a result of the products and services. Time will tell the fate of this new paradigm, but if history is any guide, success is far from assured.

None of these movements–quality, satisfaction, loyalty, etc.–is inherently flawed per se. Clearly, they all have a role in the success of a firm. The all-too-frequent failure of these management paradigms to result in improved financial performance demonstrates a more fundamental problem: their lack of a real connection to individual customer profitability.

The fact is, a satisfied, loyal customer who is persuaded to consistently buy a firm's product or service over and over again because of its quality can be and OFTEN IS unprofitable. Without an understanding of customer profitability (and the correct measurement of it), there are no goal posts to target, thus making winning (i.e., achieving profits) difficult if not impossible.

The fundamental purpose of any business is to satisfy customer wants and needs at a profit. At its most elementary level, customers are the core assets that generate a firm's profits (Gupta & Lehmann, 2003). An accurate understanding of the value of a firm's greatest assets–customers' lifetime values–can and will drive the successful management of companies in the foreseeable future.

The implications of knowing of customer lifetime value (CLV) are enormous. It will change virtually everything about the way successful businesses are managed and valued. Whether CLV is the ultimate source of competitive advantage is debatable, but one thing is certain: CLV provides meaningful goal posts to target, thus making winning possible.

REFERENCES

Bhote, K. R. (1996). *Beyond customer satisfaction to customer loyalty*. New York, NY: American Management Association.

Cigiliano, J., Georgiadis, M., Pleasance, D. & Whalley, S. (2000). The price of loyalty. *McKinsey Quarterly*.

Colby, M. (1992). Quality service manager: A new strategic direction for the '90s. *Bank Marketing (April)*, 28.

Colloquy (2005). When AIR MILES talks, we all should listen *(October 14)*, https://www.colloquy.com/

Conference Board (2002). *The CEO challenge: Top marketplace and management issues–2002*. New York.

Conference Board (2006). Customer experience management conference: Creating the right customer experiences. New York, NY (March 2-3).

Council on Financial Competition (1987). *Retail excellence: Volume 1–Service quality* (October), 3.

Crosby, P. B. (1979). *Quality is free*. New York: McGraw-Hill.

Edvardsson, B. (1988). Service quality in customer relationships: A study of critical incidents in mechanical engineering companies. *The Service Industries Journal, 8*, 4, 427-445.

Gitomer, J. (1998). *Customer satisfaction is worthless: Customer loyalty is priceless*. Marietta, GA: Bard Press.

Gordon, R. M. "Erik" (2005). A new look at customer experience. *Marketing Management, 14*, 1 (Jan/Feb), 54.

Greising, D. (1994). Quality: How to make it pay. *Business Week, 8*, 54-59.

Gupta, S. & Lehmann, D. R. (2003). Customers as assets. *Journal of Interactive Marketing, 17* (1), 9-24.

Hughes, A. M. (2002). Editorial: The mirage of CRM. *Journal of Database Management*, *9*, 2 (January), 102-104.

Keiningham, T. L. & Vavra, T. G. (2002). *The customer delight principle: Exceeding customers' expectations for bottom-line success.* New York: McGraw-Hill.

Keiningham, T. L., Vavra, T. G., Aksoy, L. & Wallard, H. (2005). *Loyalty myths: Hyped strategies that will put you out of business and proven tactics that really work.* Hoboken, NJ: John Wiley & Sons.

Levitt, T. (1960). Marketing myopia. *Harvard Business Review*, *38* (July-August), 45-56.

Parasuraman, A., Zeithaml, V. A. & Berry, L. L. (1985). A conceptual model of service quality and its implications for future research. *Journal of Marketing*, *43*, 4 (September), 41-50.

Patton, S. (2001). The truth about CRM. *CIO*, *14* (May 1), 77.

Pine, II, B. Joseph & Gilmore, J. H. (1998). Welcome to the experience economy. *Harvard Business Review*, *76*, 4 (July-August), 97-105.

Prahalad, C. K. & Ramaswamy, V. (2004). *The future of competition–Co-creating unique value with customers.* Boston MA: Harvard Business School Press.

Reichheld, F. F. (1996). *The loyalty effect.* Boston, MA: Harvard Business School Press.

Reichheld, F. F. & Sasser, W. E., Jr. (1990). Zero defections: Quality comes to services. *Harvard Business Review*, *68*, 5, 105-111.

Reinartz, W. & Kumar, V. (2002). The mismanagement of customer loyalty. *Harvard Business Review*, *80*, 7 (July), 86-94.

Schmitt, B. H. (2003). *Customer experience management: A revolutionary approach to connecting with your customers.* Hoboken, NJ: John Wiley & Sons.

White, E. (2005). Rethinking quality improvement. *Wall Street Journal* (September 19), B3.

Williams, R. & Visser, R. (2002). Customer satisfaction: It is dead but it will not lie down. *Managing Service Quality*, *12*, 3, 194-200.

doi:10.1300/J366v05n02_01

CLV:
The Databased Approach

V. Kumar

University of Connecticut

SUMMARY. It is becoming increasingly clear from the literature that there is a need for a metric that can objectively measure future profitability of the customer to the firm. This paper traces the emergence of such a metric–the customer lifetime value (CLV) and discusses the two measures of computing CLV–the aggregate approach and the individual level approach. Subsequently, eight strategies that are available to firms for maximizing CLV are discussed. These strategies assist firms in deciding how to: select the best customer, make loyal customers profitable, optimally allocate the resources, pitch the right product to the right customer at the right time, link acquisition and retention to profitability, prevent customer attrition, encourage multi-channel shopping behavior, and maximize brand value. Each of these strategies was successfully implemented by different firms across various industries, resulting in significant increases in the bottom-line. Further, the challenges in im-

---

V. Kumar (VK) is ING Chair Professor in Marketing, and Executive Director, ING Center for Financial Services, School of Business, University of Connecticut, Storrs, CT 06269-1041 (E-mail: vk@business.uconn.edu).

The author sincerely thanks the assistance of Bharath Rajan in the preparation of this document.

[Haworth co-indexing entry note]: "CLV: The Databased Approach." Kumar, V. Co-published simultaneously in *Journal of Relationship Marketing* (Best Business Books, an imprint of The Haworth Press, Inc.) Vol. 5, No. 2/3, 2006, pp. 7-35; and: *Customer Lifetime Value: Reshaping the Way We Manage to Maximize Profits* (ed: David Bejou, Timothy L. Keiningham, and Lerzan Aksoy) Best Business Books, an imprint of The Haworth Press, Inc., 2006, pp. 7-35. Single or multiple copies of this article are available for a fee from The Haworth Document Delivery Service [1-800-HAWORTH, 9:00 a.m. - 5:00 p.m. (EST). E-mail address: docdelivery@haworthpress.com].

plementing a CLV-based framework in a B-to-C organization are also discussed with an illustration. doi:10.1300/J366v05n02_02 *[Article copies available for a fee from The Haworth Document Delivery Service: 1-800-HAWORTH. E-mail address: <docdelivery@haworthpress.com> Website: <http://www.HaworthPress.com> © 2006 by The Haworth Press, Inc. All rights reserved.]*

KEYWORDS. Customer Lifetime Value, customer equity, profitability, ROI, customer loyalty, customer acquisition and retention, marketing resource allocation, brand value/brand equity, multichannel shopping, dynamic churn

INTRODUCTION

In the past two decades, the firms tended to focus on either cost management or revenue growth. When a firm adopts one of these approaches it loses out on the other (Rust, Lemon, & Zeithaml, 2004). For instance, if a firm focuses only on revenue growth without emphasis on cost management, it fails to maximize the profitability. Similarly, cost management without revenue growth affects the market performance of the firm. Therefore, balancing the two becomes essential for a firm that expects to create market-based growth while carefully evaluating profitability and return on investment (ROI) of marketing investments. In other words, the key to success lies in optimal allocation of resources/efforts across profitable customers and cost-effective customer-specific communication.

In a customer-centric approach, assessing the value of a firm's customers becomes important. But what is the value of a customer? Can customers be evaluated based only on their past contribution to the firm? Which metric is better in identifying the future worth of the customer? These are some of the questions a firm has to deal with before assessing the value of its customers. Many customer-oriented firms realize that the customers are valued more than the profit they bring in every transaction. Customers' value has to be based on their contribution to the firm across the duration of their relationship with the firm. In simple terms, the value of a customer is the value the customer brings to the firm over his/her lifetime. Some recent studies have shown that past contributions from a customer may not always reflect his or her future worth to the firm (Reinartz & Kumar, 2003). Hence, there is a need for a metric that can objectively measure future profitability of the customer to the firm (Berger & Nasr, 1998). Customer lifetime value takes into account the total financial contribution–i.e., revenues minus costs–of a customer over his or her entire lifetime with the company and therefore reflects the future profitability of the customer. *Customer lifetime value (CLV) is defined as the sum of cumulated cash flows–discounted using the Weighted Average Cost of Capital (WACC)–of a customer over his or her entire lifetime with the company.*

In this article, we first discuss the emergence and measurement of CLV. Then we find how best CLV can be used by comparing it with other traditionally used metrics. Two approaches for measuring CLV, namely the aggregate approach and the individual level approach, are explained in the following section. In the subsequent section, we discuss the strategies that can be used to maximize CLV. We also present organizational challenges in implementing CLV-based framework and we conclude the article by discussing the future of CLV.

THE EMERGENCE OF CUSTOMER LIFETIME VALUE

In order to develop and implement customized marketing strategies, it is essential for companies to understand the exact nature of the various links (e.g., strength, symmetry, and non-linearity), for efficient allocation of resources. However, owing to the complexity and specificity of the links, managers need to understand that loyalty should not be equated with higher profits.

In a series of writings, Frederick F. Reichheld stresses the importance of managing customer retention (Reichheld, Markey, & Hopton, 2000). According to his hypotheses, long-term customers tend to spend more over time, cost less to serve per period over time, have greater propensity to generate word-of-mouth and pay a premium when compared to that paid by short-term customers. Reichheld's propositions have been tested by Reinartz and Kumar who investigated the profitability of a sample of more than 16,000 individual customers across four industries (Reinartz & Kumar, 2002). The results gave a different picture. The key implication of Reinartz and Kumar's findings is that caution must be exercised when equating customer retention with customer profitability, leading to the emergence of customer lifetime value (Reinartz & Kumar, 2000). This means that firms ultimately have to make an effort to obtain information on individual or segment level profitability.

The importance of CLV rests on the fact that it is a forward-looking metric unlike other traditional measures that include past contributions to profit. It assists marketers to adopt appropriate marketing activities today, in order to increase future profitability. The computation can also be used to include prospects, not just current customers. Further, CLV is the only metric that incorporates into one, all the elements of revenue, expense and customer behavior that drive profitability. This metric also manages to score over other metrics by adopting a customer-centric approach instead of a product-centric one, as the driver of profitability. The approach for measuring CLV is given in Figure 1.

HOW CUSTOMER LIFETIME VALUE CAN BE USED

As explained earlier, CLV is a measure of the worth of a customer to the firm. Calculation of CLV for all the customers helps the firms to rank order the customers on the basis of their contribution to the firm's profits (Kumar & Reinartz, 2006). This can be the basis for formulating and implementing customer-specific strategies for maximizing their lifetime profits and increasing their lifetime duration. There are different metrics to measure and manage customer loyalty. Some of the popular metrics used are listed in Table 1.

Though RFM, Past Customer Value, and Share-of-Wallet are commonly used for computing the customer's future value, they suffer from drawbacks. These methods are not forward-looking and do not consider whether a customer is going to be active in the future. However, CLV measures consider the observed past purchase behavior and extrapolate it to the future to arrive at the future profitability of a customer. This is where the Customer Lifetime Value scores. The CLV metric helps firms

FIGURE 1. A Conceptual Approach to Measure CLV

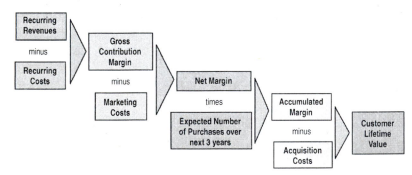

TABLE 1. Metrics Used for Measuring and Managing Customer Loyalty

Metric	Description
RFM Approach	RFM Approach stands for Recency, Frequency, and Monetary Value. Recency refers to how long it has been since a customer last placed an order with the company, frequency refers to how often a customer orders from the company in a certain defined period and monetary value denotes the amount that a customer spends on an average transaction.
Past Customer Value	It is a model that extrapolates the results of past transactions into the future. In this model, the value of a customer is determined based on the total contribution (towards profits) provided by the customer in the past.
Share of Wallet	It refers to the proportion of category value accounted for by a focal brand or a focal firm within its base of buyers. It can be measured at the individual customer level or at an aggregate level.

Source: Adapted from Kumar, V. & Reinartz, W. J. (2006). *Customer Relationship Management–A Databased Approach.* John Wiley & Sons, pp. 112-124.

address marketing issues with greater confidence. It guides the allocation of resources for ongoing marketing activities for a customer-centric firm. Kumar, Ramani, and Bohling (2004) outline these as follows:

- How do firms decide which customers should be provided with preferential and sometimes personal treatment?
- To which customers should the firms interact through inexpensive channels like the Internet or the touch tone phone, and which customer should be let go?
- How do firms decide the timing of an offering to a customer?
- How do firms decide which prospect will make a better customer in the future, and is therefore worthwhile to acquire now?
- Having got the customer to transact with the firm, what kind of sales and service resources should the firm allocate, to conduct future business with that customer?
- How should firms monitor customer activity, in order to readjust the form and intensity of their marketing initiatives?

MEASURING CUSTOMER LIFETIME VALUE

Lifetime value of a customer can be either calculated as an average CLV using an aggregate approach or individual level CLV using an individual approach.[1]

An Aggregate Approach

In the aggregate approach, average lifetime value of a customer is derived from the lifetime value of a cohort or segment or even the firm.

Three approaches to arrive at average CLV are explained here. In the first approach, the sum of lifetime values of all the customers, called Customer Equity (CE) (Kumar & Reinartz, 2006) of a firm, is calculated as:

$$CE = \sum_{i=1}^{I} \sum_{t=1}^{T} CM_{it} \left(\frac{1}{1+\delta} \right)^t \tag{1}$$

where,

CE = Customer equity of customer base in $ (sum of individual lifetime values)
CM = Net contribution margin in time period t (after taking into account the marketing costs)
δ = discount rate
i = customer index
t = time period
T = the number of time periods for which CE is being estimated.

In this case, the CE measure gives the economic value of a firm and we can calculate average CLV by dividing CE by the number of customers.

In another approach (Berger & Nasr, 1998; Kumar, Ramani, & Bohling, 2004) the average CLV of a customer is calculated from the lifetime value of a cohort or customer segment. The average CLV of a customer in the first cohort or cohort 1 can then be expressed as:

$$CLV_1 = \sum_{t=0}^{T} \left[\frac{(GC-M)}{(1+d)^t} r^t \right] - A \tag{2}$$

where,

r = rate of retention
d = discount rate or the cost of capital for the firm
t = time period
T = the number of time periods considered for estimating CE
GC = the average gross contribution
M = marketing cost per customer
A = the average acquisition cost per customer

This approach takes into account only the average gross contribution (GC), the average acquisition cost per customer (A), and marketing cost (M) per customer. The retention rate, r, is the average retention rate for the cohort and is taken as a constant over a period. However this is not the case in reality. Customers leave the relationship with the firm in different points in time therefore, the retention probabilities vary across customers. This means that we have to account for retention probabilities in the calculation for CE.

In another approach (Blattberg, Getz, & Thomas, 2001), customer equity of the firm is first calculated as the sum of return on acquisition, return on retention and return on add-on selling. This is expressed in a mathematical equation as follows;

$$(3)$$

$$CE(t) = \sum_{i=0}^{I} \left[N_{i,t}\alpha_{i,t}\left(S_{i,t}-c_{i,t}\right)-N_{i,t}B_{i,a,t} + \sum_{k=1}^{\infty} N_{i,t}\alpha_{i,t}\left(\prod_{j=1}^{k}\rho_{j,t+k}\right)\left(S_{i,t+k}-c_{i,t+k}-B_{i,r,t+k}-B_{i,AO,t+k}\right)\left(\frac{1}{1+d}\right)^{k}\right]$$

where,

$CE(t)$ = the customer equity value for customers acquired at time t
$N_{i,t}$ = the number of potential customers at time t for segment i
$\alpha_{i,t}$ = the acquisition probability at time t for segment i
$\rho_{i,t}$ = the retention probability at time t for a customer in segment i
$B_{i,a,t}$ = the marketing cost per prospect (N) for acquiring customers at time t for segment i
$B_{i,r,t}$ = the marketing in time period t for retained customers for segment i
$B_{i,AO,t}$ = the marketing costs in time period t for add-on selling for segment i
d = discount rate
$S_{i,t}$ = sales of the product/services offered by the firm at time t for segment i
$c_{i,t}$ = cost of goods at time t for segment i
I = the number of segments
I = the segment designation
t_0 = the initial time period.

Average CLV can then be arrived at by dividing CE by the number of customers.

One of the important applications of average CLV (Gupta & Lehmann, 2003; Kumar, Ramani, & Bohling, 2004) is for evaluating competitor firms. In the absence of competitors' customer level data, firms can deduce information from published financial reports about approximate gross contribution margin, marketing and advertising spending by competing firms to arrive at reasonable estimates of average CLV for competitors. This gives an idea of how profitable or unprofitable are competitors' customers. Average CLV approach can also be used for assessing the market value of the firm.

Gupta and Lehmann (2003) demonstrated that for high growth companies, aggregate CLV of a firm or customer equity may be used as a surrogate measure of firm's market value. Their approach simplifies the CLV formula, using certain assumptions. Though the computation of CLV is very easy in this approach, we can only get an approximate measure of average CLV. Since the average CLV instead of individual CLV is calculated in this method, this is considered as an aggregate approach.

However, average CLV has limited use as a metric for allocation of resources across customers because it does not capture customer level variations in CLV, which is the basis for developing customer-specific strategies. Hence it is necessary to calculate CLV of individual customers in order to design individual level strategies.

Individual-Level Approach

At an individual level, customer lifetime value is calculated as the sum of cumulated cash flows–discounted using the Weighted Average Cost of Capital (WACC)–of a customer over his or her entire lifetime with the company. It is a function of the predicted contribution margin, the propensity for a customer to continue in the relationship, and the marketing resources allocated to the customer. In its general form, CLV can be expressed as:

$$CLV_i = \sum_{t=1}^{T} \frac{(Future \text{ contribution margin}_{it} - Future \text{ cost}_{it})}{(1+d)^t} \quad (4)$$

where,

i = customer index
t = time index

T = the number of time periods considered for estimating CLV, and
d = discount rate.

The CLV has two components, future contribution margin and future
costs both adjusted for the time value of money. To calculate the future
contribution from a customer in a non-contractual setting, a firm should
know the probability that the customer continues to do business with
the firm in future time periods or probability of customer being active,
P (Active). Taking into account this probability, we can first get the
net present value (NPV) of expected Gross Contribution (EGC) as
(Reinartz & Kumar, 2003):

$$\text{NPV of EGC}_{it} = \sum_{n=t+1}^{t+x} P(Active)_{in} \times \frac{AMGC_{it}}{(1+d)^n} \qquad (5)$$

where,

$AMGC_{it}$ = average gross contribution margin in period t based on all
  prior purchases
i = customer index
t = the period for which NPV is being estimated
x = the future time period
n = the number of periods beyond t
d = Discount Rate
$P (Active)_{in}$ = the probability that customer i is active in period n

Example. The spending pattern by a customer of an IT company,
AMC Inc. is given as follows. For instance, the customer purchased a
desktop PC in January for $1,440. In the next four months he purchased
some software, flash memory, and DVDs. The average gross margin is
30% of the purchase amount and discount rate is 15% per year or 1.25%
per month. (See Table 2.)
  If the probability of customer being active, P(Active) in June is 0.40
and that in July is 0.19, then the NPV of EGC for June and July for this
customer can be calculated as follows:

AMGC = (432 + 27 + 27 + 16.2 + 10.8)/5 = 102.6

$$\qquad (6)$$

$$NPV\ of\ EGC = \left(0.4 \times \frac{57}{(1+0.125)^1}\right) + \left(0.19 \times \frac{57}{(1+0.125)^2}\right) = 28.82$$

TABLE 2. Spending Pattern of a Customer (to Calculate NPV of EGC)

	January	February	March	April	May
Purchase Amount ($)	1440	90	90	54	36
Gross Margin	432	27	27	16.2	10.8

Costs include acquisition cost (A) and the marketing costs (M) in future time periods. Marketing costs in future time period need to be discounted with appropriate discount rate, d, to arrive at the present value of these costs. The discounted marketing costs (M) and the acquisition cost (A) are then subtracted from the NPV of EGC to get the CLV of a customer. If the marketing costs are accounted at the beginning of a given time period and the gross contribution at the end of time period, we can express CLV as:

$$\text{CLV of customer } i = \sum_{n=t+1}^{t+x} P(Active)_{in} \times \frac{AMGC_{it}}{(1+d)^n} - \sum_{n=1}^{x} M_{in} \times \left(\frac{1}{1+d}\right)^{n-1} - A$$

Average monthly gross contribution (AMGC). The average monthly gross contribution, AMGC, is the average monthly revenue obtained from a customer minus the average cost of goods sold. This is calculated based on his/her past purchases.

Marketing cost (M). This includes the development and retention costs. It can be the cost of programs to increase the value of existing relationship, cost of loyalty or frequent flyer programs, cost of campaigns to "win back" the lost customers, and the cost of serving the customer accounts. One main component of these costs is the cost of marketing contacts through various channels of communication. The contacts through different channels have different costs to the firm. For example, a face-to-face meeting with customer costs much higher than communication through direct mail or e-mail. To arrive at marketing costs specific to a customer, firms need to estimate the number of contacts required to retain the customer and the cost of contact through various channels. Once firms have such cost accounting, calculation of marketing cost is straightforward. Estimation of marketing cost is important in arriving at optimal customer specific communication strategies.

Discount rate (d). The revenue or gross contribution from the customer comes at different time periods in the future, accounted yearly, monthly, or weekly. The value of money is not constant across time and since the money received today is more valuable than that received in future time periods, the GC and marketing costs have to be discounted to the present value of money. This is achieved by dividing the cash flow in time period i by $(1 + d)^i$, where d is the discount rate. The discount rate, d, depends on the general rate of interest and is normally proportional to the Treasury bill or the interest that banks pay on savings accounts. It can also vary across firms depending upon the cost of capital to the firm.

Time period (n). The number of future time periods (n) for which the gross contribution and the marketing costs are considered for calculation of CLV refers to the natural "lifetime" of the customers. For most businesses it is reasonable to expect that the customers will return for a number of years (n). There are no strict guidelines to decide on the value of n. The word "lifetime" must be taken in many circumstances with a grain of salt. While the term makes little sense with one-off purchases (say, for example, a house), it also seems strange to talk about LTV of a grocery shopper. Clearly, there is an actual lifetime value of a grocery shopper. However, given the long time span, this actual value has not much practical value. For all practical purposes, the lifetime duration is a longer-term duration that is managerially useful. For example, in a direct marketing general merchandise context, managers consider maximum four-year time span, sometimes only two years. Beyond that, any calculation and prediction may become difficult due to so many uncontrollable factors (the customer moves, a new competitor moves in, and so on). It is therefore important to make an educated judgment as to what is a sensible duration horizon in the context of making decisions.

P (Active) $_{in}$ is the probability that the customer continues to be active in subsequent time period. For CLV calculation to be at an individual level, this probability of retaining customer has to be calculated at an individual customer level rather than the average rate of retention at the firm level. Each customer is likely to have different purchase patterns and his/her active and inactive periods vary as shown in the following Figure 2.

Given their purchase behavior in the past, one can predict the probability of individual customers being active or P (Active) in subsequent time periods. A simple formula to calculate P (Active) is

$$P(Active) = (T/N)^n \tag{8}$$

Where n is the number of purchases in the observation period, T is the time elapsed between acquisition and the most recent purchase, and N is

FIGURE 2. Variations in Inter-Purchase Time

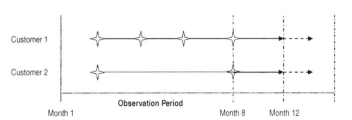

the time elapsed between acquisition and the period for which P (*Active*) needs to be determined. For illustration, if ✧ indicates a purchase, then for customer 1,

P (*Active*) in month 12 = $(8/12)^4$ = 0.197 where n = number of purchase = 4

P (*Active*) for customer 2 in month 12 = $(8/12)^2$ = 0.444 where n = 2

In the above case, for a customer who bought four times in the first eight months and did not buy in the next four months, the probability of purchase after four months (i.e., at the end of month 12) is less than that of customer 2 who purchased only two times in the first eight months. The formula introduced here for calculation of P (Active) is very basic. However, other sophisticated methods are employed for the calculation of the probability of a customer purchasing in future time periods.

One drawback of using P (Active) to predict customers' future activity is that it assumes that when a customer terminates a relationship, he/she does not come back to the firm. This approach called "lost-for-good" is questionable because it systematically underestimates CLV (Rust, Lemon, & Zeithaml, 2004). To overcome this, researchers use "always-a-share" approach, which takes into account the possibility of a customer returning to the supplier after a temporary dormancy in a relationship (Venkatesan & Kumar, 2004). In this case, predicting the frequency of a customer's purchases given his or her previous purchase is a better way of projecting future customer activity. This predicted frequency can be used to calculate CLV. The CLV function which incorporates predicted frequency can be expressed as follows;

$$CLV_i = \sum_{y=1}^{T_i} \frac{CM_{i,y}}{(1+d)^{y/frequency_i}} - \sum_{l=1}^{n} \frac{\sum_m c_{i,m,l} \times x_{i,m,l}}{(1+d)^l} \qquad (9)$$

where,

CLV_i = lifetime value of customer i,
$CM_{i,y}$ = predicted contribution margin from customer i in purchase occasion y,
d = discount rate,
$c_{i,m,l}$ = unit marketing cost for customer i in channel m in year l,
$x_{i,m,l}$ = number of contacts to customer i in channel m in year l,
$frequency_i$ = predicted purchase frequency for customer i,
n = number of years to forecast, and
T_i = predicted number of purchases made by customer i until the end of planning period.

Example. Suppose the predicted contribution from a customer in purchase occasions in next two years, number of marketing contacts and the marketing costs in different channels are as shown in Table 3. Predicted purchase frequency = 3

$$CLV = \frac{170}{(1+0.15)^{1/3}} + \dots + \frac{51}{(1+0.15)^{6/3}} - \left\{ (2.5\times4) + 3\times2 + \frac{(2.5\times4)+(3\times3)}{(1+0.15)} \right\} = \$630.20 \qquad (10)$$

Various supplier-specific factors (channel communication) and customer characteristics (involvement, switching costs, and previous behavior) are first identified as the antecedents of purchase frequency and contribution margin. Purchase frequency and contribution margin are then modeled separately using suitable models. In the framework devel-

TABLE 3. Predicted Contribution from a Customer

Time Period	Jan '05	May '05	Nov '05	Feb '06	Jul '06	Oct '06
Predicted Contribution ($)	170	119	85	153	110.5	51

Number of direct mails: Year 1 = 4   Year 2 = 4
Number of contacts via telephone: Year 1 = 2   Year 2 = 3
Cost per direct mail ($)   2.50
Cost per contact via telephone ($) 3.00
If the discount rate is taken as 15%, then CLV of this customer can be calculated as given in equation 10.

oped by Venkatesan and Kumar (2004), a generalized gamma distribution is used to model inter-purchase time, and panel-data regression methodologies are employed in modeling the contribution margin.

The CLV model described can be employed to identify the responsiveness of customers to marketing communication through different channels of communication, which is the basis for optimal allocation of marketing resources across channels of contact for each customer so as to maximize his or her respective CLVs. In addition to using the CLV framework for resource allocation strategy, it can also be used for formulating other customer-level strategies such as customer selection, purchase sequence analysis, and for targeting right customers for acquisition.

As can be seen from the CLV calculations, the lifetime value of a customer depends to a great extent on whether the customer is going to be active in the future time periods or not. This is especially important in a non-contractual setting because customer has the freedom to leave the relationship any time. Hence it is very important for a firm to understand the factors influencing the profitable duration of customer with the firm or the drivers of profitable lifetime duration.

STRATEGIES TO MAXIMIZE CUSTOMER LIFETIME VALUE

Once the computation of CLV is completed, firms must look forward to maximize it in order to reap the full benefits of the metric. In recent years, managers have tried to measure and maximize the lifetime value of each and every customer. If a company truly understood each customer's lifetime value, it could maximize its own value by boosting the number, scope and duration of value-creating customer relationships. Some cutting-edge marketing strategies that are available for maximizing customer lifetime value are listed in Figure 3.

Description of Strategies

Each of these strategies plays a unique role in optimizing shareholder value, customer equity, and overall profitability. Each strategy also works in combination with other strategies to increase the overall impact on the firm value. These strategies will be discussed using recent research in marketing and successful implementations for businesses within various industries (both business to consumer [B2C] and business to business [B2B]).

FIGURE 3. Overview of Strategies

Strategies	What They Do
Selecting the Best Customer	To detect and target customers/distributors based on their value potential.
Making Loyal Customers Profitable	For efficient allocation of resources and an increase in profitability, a segmentation approach is undertaken.
Optimally Allocating the Resources	Used in designing the optimal marketing spend across channels.
Pitching Right Product to the Right Customer at the Right Time	Firms send out sales and promotion messages to their customers that are relevant to the products that are more likely to be purchased next. This way the firm does not waste or duplicate its sales and marketing efforts.
Linking Acquisition and Retention Resources to Profitability	Targeting prospects and retaining profitable ones would result in efficient allocation of marketing budget and maximizes profitability.
Preventing Customer Attrition	Help firms decide which customer/distributor is likely to quit and at what time.
Encouraging Multi-channel Shopping Behavior	Used to migrate low-value customers/distributors to low cost channels based on purchase behavior.
Maximizing Brand Value	To manage individual customer brand value and maximize customer lifetime value, brand value is linked to CLV.

Selecting the Best Customer

The objective of customer selection is to detect and target customers/distributors based on their value potential as opposed to other traditional metrics like RFM, Past Customer Value and Share of Wallet (Reinartz & Kumar, 2003). Customer selection strategies are applied when firms want to target individual customers or groups of customers. The reasons for targeting these customers can be manifold and finding the right targets for marketing resource allocation is at the heart of any CRM strategy. One step in the successful implementation of CRM is the smart deployment of targeting methodologies so as to maximize the benefits to the firm and the customer (Venkatesan & Kumar, 2004). The benefit of selecting the top 20% of the customers using a CLV score versus the traditional metrics, is that the average revenue for a customer selected on the basis of CLV is about 60% greater than customers selected using other metrics.

Making Loyal Customers Profitable

For managing loyalty and profitability simultaneously, a segmentation-based approach is used that would guide marketing actions to loyal customers/distributors (Kumar & Shah, 2004). Figure 4 illustrates the analysis for making loyal customers profitable.

The four quadrants of the matrix suggests how customers can be sorted on the basis of customer longevity and profitability for the firm. While there may be long-standing customers who are only marginally

FIGURE 4. Making Loyal Customers Profitable

	BUTTERFLIES	TRUE FRIENDS

High Profitability	• Good fit of company offering and customer needs
	• High profit potential
	• Actions:
	  - Aim to achieve transactional satisfaction, not attitudinal loyalty
	  - Milk the accounts as long as they are active
	  - Key challenge: cease investment once inflection point is reached
		• Good fit of company offering and customer needs
		• Highest profit potential
		• Actions:
		  - Consistent intermittently-spaced communication
		  - Achieve attitudinal *and* behavioral loyalty
		  - Delight to nuture/defend/retain

	STRANGERS	BARNACLES

Low Profitability	• Little fit of company offering and customer needs
	• Lowest profit potential
	• Action:
	  - No relationship investment
	  - Profitize every transaction
		• Limited fit of company offering and customer needs
		• Low profit potential
		• Action:
		  - Measure size and share-of-wallet
		  - If share-of-wallet is low, specific up-selling and cross-selling
		  - If size of wallet it small, strict cost control

Short-term Customers   Long-term Customers

profitable, there may be short-term customers who are highly profitable. Hence it becomes clear that, the relationship between loyalty and profitability is by no means assured.

True Friends are the most valuable customers of all. They fit in well with the company offerings. They are also steady purchasers, buying regularly, but not intensively, over time. They offer the highest profit potential for the firm. In managing these true friends, firms should indulge in consistent, yet intermittently spaced communication. Firms should strive to achieve attitudinal *and* behavioural loyalty among these customers.

Butterflies are customers who, though staying for only a short term, offer high profitability for the firm. They enjoy finding out the best deals, and avoid building a stable relationship with any single provider. So, firms should stop investing in these customers once the activity drops. Managers should look for ways to enjoy them while they can and find the right moment to cease investing in them. Hence, in order to manage this type of customers, firms should aim to achieve transactional satisfaction, and *not* attitudinal loyalty.

Barnacles are those customers who, in spite of being long-term customers, offer low profitability for the firm. They are a limited fit for the company, provide low profit potential and do not generate satisfactory return on investments due to their small size and low volume of transactions. Like barnacles on the hull of a cargo ship, they only create additional drag. However, when properly managed, they can become profitable. To manage this type of customer, firms should determine whether the problem is a small wallet or a small share of the wallet. If the share-of-wallet is low, specific up-selling and cross-selling can be done to extract profitability. However, if the size of wallet is small, then strict cost control measures have to be implemented to reduce loss for the firm.

Strangers, as the name suggests, are the least profitable customers for the firm. They fit in poorly with the company offerings. To manage these customers, the key is to identify them early and refrain from making any relationship investment. These customers have no loyalty towards the firm and bring in no profits. Hence, every transaction with the strangers should be profitable.

While designing and implementing loyalty programs, care has to be exercised in deciding the focus of the loyalty programs. Past and present research findings, coupled with advances in database management technologies, have all contributed towards the emergence of a new dominant-logic paradigm of customer loyalty programs that is characterized by "personalization" and "customization" at individual customer level. The benefit of switching to such a customer-centric program is that the newly defined loyal customers will be profitable customers. Table 4 summarizes the changes in dimensions of customer loyalty programs that seem to evince a discernible evolving dominant logic.

Optimally Allocating the Resources

Choosing the right channel and expending the right amount of resources is essential for a firm to improve its results. Venkatesan and Kumar (2004) have developed a framework that enables firms to determine optimal marketing strategies across various channels to each customer within the database, while at the same time continuing to maximize financial performance of the firm. In adopting this method, Venkatesan and Kumar were able to show significant gains in profitability for a multinational B2B firm. Further, they found this optimization of marketing resources caused the amount spent on contacting customers to increase significantly over the next three years. This proves that maximizing profitability and optimizing marketing resources does not necessarily mean cutting back on the marketing budget; it just means that revenues need to increase faster than costs. Figure 5 explains the effects of opti-

TABLE 4. Changes in Customer Loyalty Programs

No.	Dimension	Earlier Loyalty Programs: Program Centric	Evolving Loyalty Programs: Customer Centric
1	Operationalization Level	Aggregate Level	Customer Level
2	Program Type	Standardized, based on usage or spend.	Customized, based on type of usage or type of spend.
3	Rewarding Scheme	Standard and uniform aimed at repeat purchase.	Personalized and relevant, aimed at influencing specific behavioral change or attitudinal gratification.
4	Reward Options	Minimal	Multiple (usually made possible through partners and alliances).
5	Reward Mechanism	Reactive	Reactive + Proactive
6	Reward Type	Tangible	Tangible + Experiential
7	Program Objective	Build market share, increase revenues, Build behavioral loyalty through repeat purchase or usage.	Link loyalty to profitability, Influence behavioral loyalty, Cultivate attitudinal loyalty.
8	Metrics Used	RFM, Past Customer Value (PCV), Share of Wallet (SOW)	Customer Lifetime Value (CLV)
9	Technology & Analytics Usage	Minimal	Extensive

Kumar, V. & Shah, D. (2004). Building and Sustaining Profitable Customer Loyalty for the 21st Century. *Journal of Retailing*, Vol. 80 (4), pp. 326. Printed with permission © New York University.

mal resource allocation strategy on a contact strategy within a B2B company.

The optimal resource allocation strategy enables the firm to take specific marketing actions for a larger set of customers/distributors, for a given budget. It provides the firm with the framework to assess return on its marketing investments and hence bring accountability to marketing actions. While contacting the right customers using the right amount of resources continues to increase the profitability and the performance of the firm, it is still possible to refine the marketing strategy further and determine what exactly the customers are looking to buy and when they might be purchasing each type of product or service.

Pitching Right Product to the Right Customer at the Right Time

Most firms offer a range of products. A customer who has bought a particular product is unlikely to buy the same product immediately. It would be useful for a firm to predict the relative probabilities of different product categories being bought at different times from a given firm, given the varying purchase patterns of each of its customers. This would mean contacting customers at appropriate time intervals, about products they are more likely to buy, resulting in a more focused approach.

FIGURE 5. Optimal Resource Allocation Strategy

Share of Wallet

	Low	High
Low	Face to Face Meetings: Currently every 6.9 months Optimally every 11.4 months Direct Mail/Telesales: Current interval is 33 days Optimal interval is 61 days	Face to Face Meetings: Currently every 4.2 months Optimally every 6.6 months Direct Mail/Telesales: Current interval is 21 days Optimal interval is 49 days
High	Face to Face Meetings: Currently every 6.7 months Optimally every 3.9 months Direct Mail/Telesales: Current interval is 31 days Optimal interval is 18 days	Face to Face Meetings: Currently every 4.2 months Optimally every 2.4 months Direct Mail/Telesales: Current interval is 22 days Optimal interval is 13 days

Customer Value (vertical axis label for rows)

A purchase sequence model can be developed that captures the differences in the durations between purchases for different product categories by incorporating cross-product category variables. After recording the interdependence in purchase propensities across product categories as well as in the purchase timing, customer level predictions can be developed to target the right customer, with the right product at the right time. The results of the purchase sequence model can be evaluated using test and control groups. Using the purchase sequence model with customer data from a B2B firm, Kumar, Venkatesan, and Reinartz (2006) were able to show 180% more ROI for the study using this model, over the traditional models.

By understanding the purchase sequence, firms can target the right product to the right customer at the right time. It helps in increasing cross-buy ratio and revenue, apart from decreasing marketing costs, thereby leading to an incremental ROI. This also helps firms to devise effective cross-sell and up-sell strategies. This, when integrated with CLV measure, can help companies design the most optimal marketing strategy directed towards offering the right product to the right customer at the right time through the most cost-effective channel.

Linking Acquisition and Retention Resources to Profitability

Linking acquisition and retention to profitability is used to target profitable prospects and retain profitable customers/distributors (Reinartz, Thomas, & Kumar, 2005). This approach traces the drivers of the three constructs, viz., acquisition likelihood, relationship duration and customer profitability. The drivers include actions undertaken by the firm, customer and competitors. With the help of these drivers, a manager should increase the acquisition likelihood of a prospect, relationship duration and customer profitability.

The resource allocation decisions fall into two categories–offensive marketing and defensive marketing. While offensive marketing involves strategies that are designed to obtain additional customers and encourage brand switching, defensive marketing strategies are designed to reduce customer exits and brand switching. A point to be noted here is that resources have to be allocated to both kinds of strategies simultaneously. There exists a conceptual link between the offensive process and the defensive process. A failure to link acquisition and retention can lead to biased results and incorrect inferences resulting from the omission of information on non-acquired prospects. Since offensive processes and defensive processes compete for the same resources, making the necessary tradeoff requires a full specification of the key dimensions of the customer-firm relationship. The link allows managers to examine whether the maximization of the objective functions for acquisition likelihood, relationship duration, and customer profitability lead to convergent or divergent resource allocation recommendations.

This model incorporates profitability into marketing-mix decisions, revealing how much companies must spend on direct marketing to maximize profitability and how they should most profitably allocate that spending. Thomas, Reinartz, and Kumar (2004) were able to increase profits for a B2B, a pharmaceutical firm and a catalog retailer, by an average of 35% by optimally directing its marketing expenditures. In addition to this, it was shown that about 28% of the firm's profits are from 27% of loyal customers (who are high cost to acquire and retain). Thus, firms need to carefully pick customers in each of the four cells to maximize financial performance.

Preventing Customer Attrition

The dynamic churn models help decide which customer/distributor is likely to quit and at what time. This results in an increase in ROI due to "timely" marketing intervention. Some of the strategic questions involving managers are

- Should we intervene?
- Which customers to intervene?
- When to intervene?

- Through which channel to intervene? and
- What to offer?

The solution for these questions lies in building propensity-to-quit models and integrating them with the CLV-based models. So, it becomes essential on the part of the managers to study the customer quitting tendencies. For instance, consider three customers–Customer A, Customer B and Customer C. Their predicted propensity to quit over time (July 2004 to July 2005) is illustrated in Figure 6. Accordingly, Customer A does not intend to quit and is denoted by a straight line. Customer B, though not exhibiting a quitting tendency initially, shows an increase in propensity to quit from January 2005. Customer C, represented by a steep line, shows a strong tendency to quit from early on. Clearly, this indicates that Customers B and C are likely to quit in the near future and they are the customers to be intervened.

Once the need to intervene and the customers to be intervened has been decided, firms have to identify when the intervention has to be made. The answer to this question lies with a proactive intervention strategy. That is, the customers who show a strong tendency to quit (in this case Customers B and C) should be intervened by the firm to prevent customer attrition. Figure 7 shows the time periods in which Customers B and C are intervened.

In Figure 7, points I_1 and I_2 denote the intervention points when customers B and C should be intervened and this is followed by a decrease in propensity to quit on the part of the customers. Here, Customer B is

FIGURE 6. Predicting Propensity to Quit

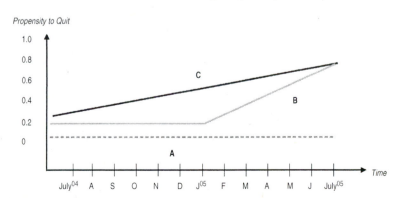

FIGURE 7. Proactive Intervention Strategy

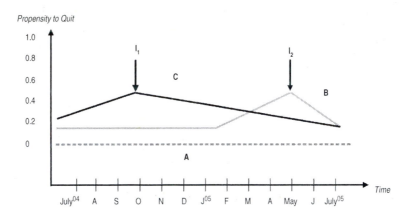

being intervened in April 2005 and Customer C in October 2004. The reason for the time lag between the customer intervention stems from their respective propensities to quit. So, while Customer C has to be intervened early on, Customer B can be intervened at a later stage. The decision on the channel of intervention and the offer through which the intervention is to be made can be decided by the companies based on individual customer characteristics. Thus, proactive intervention strategies help companies to preempt customer attrition and thereby increase ROI. In implementing this framework for a B2C IT firm, we were able to reduce the churn by 30% and increase the profits by 42%.

Encouraging Multi-Channel Shopping Behavior

Multi-channel analysis is used to migrate low-value customers/distributors to low-cost channels based on purchase behavior. It has been found that, at least in the B2B setting, multi-channel shoppers provide better benefits than single-channel shoppers (Kumar & Venkatesan, 2005). Figure 8 explains the drivers of multi-channel shopping and behavioral characteristics of multi-channel shoppers.

This implies that multi-channel shoppers differ from single-channel shoppers in having a deeper relationship, a greater trust and offer lower perceived risk in their transactions. The drivers of multi-channel shopping can be classified into customer characteristics, supplier-specific factors and customer demographics. Customer characteristics include

FIGURE 8. Drivers of Multi-Channel Shopping and Behavioral Characteristics of Multi-Channel Shoppers

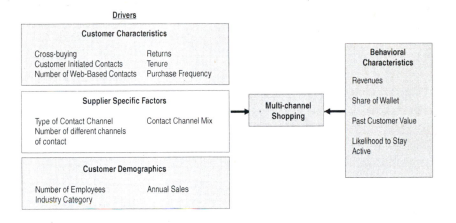

factors such as cross-buying, returns, frequency of web-based contacts, tenure of the customer with the firm, and frequency of customer purchases. In other words, the higher the frequency of these factors the more is the likelihood of multi-channel shopping. The supplier-specific factors include the number of different channels used for contact, type of contact channel and channel mix. Here again, the more the degree of supplier specific factors, the more the likelihood of multi-channel shopping. The customer demographics refer to number of employees in the firm serving customers, annual sales of the firm and the industry category. The behavioral characters refer to customer-based metrics including revenues, past customer value, share of wallet and predicted propensity to stay in relationship.

The strategic issues concerning multi-channel analysis involve questions such as

- Should multi-channel shopping be encouraged?
- Does it matter what the second channel is?
- What should the migration pattern of customers be? and
- Can migration be influenced?

The channel migration campaigns should target customers who provide higher gross profits, purchase across product categories, and transact frequently with the firm. Kumar and Venkatesan (2005) show that shoppers who buy across every available channel tend to initiate more contact with the firm, have a longer tenure with the firm, make more frequent purchases, be more active with the firm, and provide higher revenues. For instance, the mean revenue ($60,076) for customers who shop in four channels was significantly different and larger from the mean revenue of each of the other customers who shop across only one ($4,262), two ($5,736), or three channels ($13,250).

Maximizing Brand Value

Linking brand value to CLV is used for managing individual customer brand value. This results in maximizing customer lifetime value. The link between Individual Brand Value (IBV) and Customer Lifetime Value (CLV) is established in a series of steps, as illustrated in Figure 9.

In the first step, the CLV of the customer base is measured. The second step involves customer selection. Here, the customers are ranked based on their CLV, and a sample (10% of each decile) is generated so that a database with high variation in CLV is obtained. Thirdly, for the set of customers, the measurements for the individual's brand values are obtained. These individual brand values include constructs such as awareness of the brand, perceived image of the brand, trust, emotional attachment towards the brand, loyalty towards the brand, advocacy of the brand to others, and regular purchases made. In the next step, the IBV is linked to the CLV. In other words, the customer's computed lifetime value is expressed as a function of values of individual brand pref-

FIGURE 9. Managing an Individual's Brand Value and Customer Lifetime Value

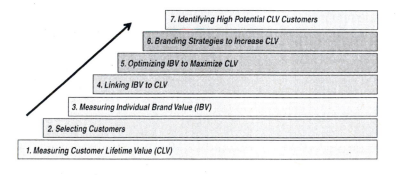

erences that were obtained in step three. Then, the IBV and CLV optimization is done. Here, the measurements of the individual's brand value are optimized to maximize the customer's CLV. Then, the optimized individual brand values are translated to brand management strategies, and the success of brand management strategies are measured at an individual level based on CLV. Finally, the potential customers are targeted by prioritizing and selecting customers based on CLV and by identifying valuable potential customers based on the profiling of existing high CLV customers. The CLV driven by a potential customer's brand value is calculated by estimating brand knowledge, brand attitude and brand behavior intention of the potential customer. Kumar and Luo found that by increasing the brand value score for a set of customers resulted in an increase in CLV of over 34% for a B2B IT firm.

IMPLEMENTING CLV FRAMEWORK IN A B-TO-C ORGANIZATION

Collection of transaction data for all the end consumers poses a great challenge for a B-to-C organization. The data collection can be very expensive because of relatively large numbers of customers. In some cases getting transaction data on all the customers is impossible because the firm is not in direct contact with the end-consumers. This is true in the case of an FMCG manufacturer who sells through the intermediary channels. In such cases, the computation and application of CLV need to be modified to make maximum use of the framework. This can be illustrated using the following case studies.

Case Study 1: CLV Framework Applied to Software Manufacturer

A software manufacturer who sells through intermediaries has limited information about the transactions by the end consumers. In this case, the manufacturer cannot calculate the value of the end consumer using the data available with the company. Instead, it can rely on survey data. Company can conduct a survey of a large number of end consumers (say 2000) and collect information on what products and upgrades have been bought by each customer in the past, and their demographic/firmographic variables. This gives us information on transactions for consumers in the sample. Based on this information, the firm can calculate the value of each customer. For example, survey data gives us a measure of purchase frequency, measure of purchase value and thereby a measure of the contribution margin, types of products purchased and marketing costs. Marketing cost in this case may not be available at an individual customer level. However, the firm can allocate mass communication costs to individual customer level. The basis for allocation can be either the share value of purchase or the contribution. Based on this information, the firm can make projections on future frequencies, contribution margin and market costs, and assess the value of the customer. Once the customer values are calculated, the customers can be grouped into deciles or segments based on the customer value. The firm can then profile the customers in different segments/deciles. This will help the firm to identify the profile of high value customers. The firm can therefore identify high potential customers who have matching profiles with existing high value customers and create marketing strategy to reach out to these prospects. This will ensure targeting and acquiring prospects who have high customer lifetime value which in turn will help to maximize the customer equity of the firm.

Case Study 2: CLV Framework Applied to Soft Drink Manufacturer

A soft drink manufacturer usually sells through its intermediary channels. Though the company may have the data on sales to its intermediaries, it is unlikely to have transaction data for all the end consumers. Also, the number of end-consumers will be unmanageably large. The contribution from each customer may be low and hence managing business at an individual level may not be the right strategy because of high touch cost relative to the contribution from an individual customer. Instead, the firm will be interested in knowing the drivers of consumption at different age groups so that it can improve the drivers of CLV to maximize the customer value from that age group (Kumar & George, 2005). In order to identify the drivers, the firm needs to gather information on consumption and demographic variables from a large number of respondents from different age groups.

For example, customers can first be divided into various groups. Then, a random sample of customers within each group for all the age groups can be selected. From these selections, information about the quantity of soft drink (specific brand) consumed by each respondent, and the demographic variables can be collected using a questionnaire survey. Based on this data the firm can arrive at a rough estimate of the lifetime value of a customer in each age group. However, the average consumption and the variation within each age segment may vary. This study will help us to understand how the average yearly consumption varies across different age groups and the variation within each age group. If a firm computes the average yearly consumption of a specific brand of soft drink for different age groups, it can calculate the total consumption of that brand of soft drink by an average consumer in his/her lifetime.

However, the variation in consumption within an age group may be high. Therefore the average consumption will not help us in developing strategies for the age segments. Instead, the firm should identify the demographic variables which explain the variation in consumption pattern of customers within an age group either by regressing the average monthly consumption quantity on different demographic variables or by using other suitable statistical techniques. The average monthly consumption quantity (CQ) can be expressed as a function of demographic variables as given below:

$$(11)$$

$$CQ_i = f(Age, Education, Income, Occupation, Gender, Ethnicity, Religion, \ldots)$$

These drivers of consumption pattern help the firm to predict the lifetime value of customers in that age group across a heterogeneous group of individuals. Firms can then formulate a suitable marketing strategy for each age group to maximize customer value from each age group. It can make use of publicly available data such as census to collect information on demographic variables of customers in different age groups of the population. Such information along with the drivers of lifetime value can be used to predict the lifetime value of customers in each group (i.e., total of lifetime values of all the customers in that segment). This will help the firm to direct its marketing efforts to the high value customer segment. It can also use the profile information of high value customer groups to target high potential prospects. These strategies collectively will maximize the customer equity of the firm.

FUTURE OF CLV

CLV framework relies on customers' personal and behavioral information. Firms, while gathering and using customer-level information, should be aware of the privacy issues and take steps to gain the confidence of customers. CLV framework is also expected to undergo further sophistication and improvement. Improvements are expected in (1) measuring CLV, (2) a better understanding of the antecedents or drivers of CLV, and (3) emergence of evidence regarding the importance of using CLV as the metric for Resource Allocation.

The formula for calculation of CLV has improved in the past two years significantly. However, considering the dynamic nature of the purchase behavior of customers, more sophisticated models that incorporate the conditional effects of changes in the amount and quality of marketing mix need to be developed (Reinartz & Kumar, 2003). The future models are also expected to incorporate the impact of Word-of-Mouth in determining the lifetime value of customers. Another area of improvement is expected in identification of other meaningful antecedents of CLV in addition to the ones discussed in this article. With more and more firms adopting CLV framework for resource allocation and other customer-specific strategies, CLV is expected to gain widespread acceptability as the preferred metric for resource allocation.

NOTE

1. For a detailed discussion on this topic, kindly refer to Kumar, V. "Customer Lifetime Value," forthcoming, *Handbook of Marketing Research*, Sage Publications.

REFERENCES

Berger, P. D. & Nasr, Nada I. (1998). Customer Lifetime Value: Marketing Models and Applications. *Journal of Interactive Marketing, 12,* 17-30.

Blattberg, R. C., Getz G., & Thomas J. S. (2001). Customer Equity: Building and Managing Relationships as Valuable Assets. *Harvard Business School Press.*

Gupta, S. & Lehmann, D. R. (2003). Customer as Assets. *Journal of Interactive Marketing, 17*(1), 9-24.

Kumar, V. & George, M. (2005). A Comparison of Aggregate and Disaggregate Level Approaches for Measuring and Maximizing Customer Equity. Working paper, University of Connecticut.

Kumar, V. & Luo, M. Linking an Individual's Brand Value to the CLV: An Integrated Framework. Working Paper, University of Connecticut.

Kumar, V., Ramani, G. & Bohling, T. (2004). Customer lifetime Value Approaches and Best Practices Applications. *Journal of Interactive Marketing, 3,* 60-72.

Kumar, V. & Reinartz, W. J. (2006). *Customer Relationship Management–A Databased Approach* (1st ed.). New York: John Wiley & Sons.

Kumar, V. & Shah, D. (2004). Building and Sustaining Profitable Customer Loyalty for the 21st Century. *Journal of Retailing, 80*(4), 317-330.

Kumar, V. & Venkatesan, R. (2005). Who Are the Multi-Channel Shoppers and How Do They Perform?: Correlates of multi-channel shopping behavior. *Journal of Interactive Marketing, 19,* 44-62.

Kumar, V., Venkatesan R., & Reinartz, W. J. (2006). Knowing What to Sell When to Whom. *Harvard Business Review,* forthcoming.

Reichheld, F. F., Markey, R. G., Jr., & Hopton, C. (2000). The Loyalty Effect–The Relationship Between Loyalty and Profits. *European Business Journal, 12,* 134.

Reinartz, W. J. & Kumar, V. (2000). On the Profitability of Long-Life Customers in a Non-Contractual Setting: An Empirical Investigation and Implications for Marketing. *Journal of Marketing, 64,* 17-32.

Reinartz, W. J. & Kumar, V. (2002). The Mismanagement of Customer Loyalty. *Harvard Business Review, 7,* 86.

Reinartz, W. J. & Kumar, V. (2003). The Impact of Customer Relationship Characteristics on Profitable Lifetime Duration. *Journal of Marketing, 67*(1), 77-99.

Reinartz, W., Thomas, J., & Kumar, V. (2005). Balancing Acquisition and Retention Resources to Maximize Profitability. *Journal of Marketing, 69,* 63-79.

Rust, R. T., Lemon, K. N., & Zeithaml, V. A. (2004). Return on Marketing: Using Customer Equity to Focus Marketing Strategy. *Journal of Marketing, 68,* 109-127.

Thomas, J., Reinartz, W. J., & Kumar, V. (2004). Getting the Most out of All Your Customers. *Harvard Business Review,* 116-123.

Venkatesan, R. & Kumar, V. (2004). A Customer Lifetime Value Framework for Customer Selection and Optimal Resource Allocation Strategy. *Journal of Marketing, 68*(4), 106-125.

doi:10.1300/J366v05n02_02

Approaches to the Measurement and Management of Customer Value

Timothy L. Keiningham

Ipsos Loyalty

Lerzan Aksoy

Koc University, Istanbul, Turkey

David Bejou

Virginia State University

SUMMARY. Determining and managing customer lifetime value is one of the most important strategic objectives of companies today. This paper critically examines some of the most popular approaches traditionally used to measure the value of customers in a company's portfolio. The methods reviewed include RFM and total revenue ap-

Timothy L. Keiningham, MBA, is Senior Vice President and Head of Consulting, Ipsos Loyalty, Morris Corporation Center 2, 1 Upper Pond Road, Building D, Parsippany, NJ 07054 (E-mail: tim.keiningham@ipsos-na.com).

Lezran Aksoy, PhD, is Assistant Professor of Marketing, Koc University, College of Administrative Sciences and Economics, Rumeli Feneri Yolu, Sariyer 80910 Istanbul, Turkey (E-mail: laksoy@ku.edu.tr).

David Bejou, PhD, is Dean, School of Business, Virginia State University, P.O. Box 9398, Petersburg, VA 23806 (E-mail: dbejou@vsu.edu).

[Haworth co-indexing entry note]: "Approaches to the Measurement and Management of Customer Value." Keiningham, Timothy L., Lerzan Aksoy, and David Bejou. Co-published simultaneously in *Journal of Relationship Marketing* (Best Business Books, an imprint of The Haworth Press, Inc.) Vol. 5, No. 2/3, 2006, pp. 37-54; and: *Customer Lifetime Value: Reshaping the Way We Manage to Maximize Profits* (ed: David Bejou, Timothy L. Keiningham, and Lerzan Aksoy) Best Business Books, an imprint of The Haworth Press, Inc., 2006, pp. 37-54. Single or multiple copies of this article are available for a fee from The Haworth Document Delivery Service [1-800-HAWORTH, 9:00 a.m. - 5:00 p.m. (EST). E-mail address: docdelivery@haworthpress.com].

Available online at http://jrm.haworthpress.com
doi:10.1300/J366v05n02_03

proaches to differentiating the value of customers. Although these methods have relative advantages, they have serious drawbacks that limit the ability of managers to accurately assess customer value. An alternative model for the measurement and management of customer value is proposed. doi:10.1300/J366v05n02_03 *[Article copies available for a fee from The Haworth Document Delivery Service: 1-800-HAWORTH. E-mail address: <docdelivery@haworthpress.com> Website: <http://www.HaworthPress.com> © 2006 by The Haworth Press, Inc. All rights reserved.]*

KEYWORDS. Customer lifetime value, customer profitability, RFM

Looking back at thought-leading articles on management over the last half century, one common theme becomes incontestably apparent. Virtually each successive year can be legitimately described as the most competitive business environment in history.

The result has been the decline and fall of time-honored, respected firms both large and small . . . even those with throngs of loyal customers. As a result, Joseph Schumpeter's (1942) theory of "creative destruction" often appears more like "chaotic demolition." Hence, it is not difficult to find articles like the following:

- "Broke But Beloved," which begins "Say this for WINfirst, the troubled cable, telephone and Internet provider: It has very loyal customers. Since filing for Chapter 11 bankruptcy protection in March . . ." (Shallit Bob, 2002);
- "With competitive prices, loyal customers and fast-loading Web pages showing 100,000 toys and children's goods, eToys Inc. looked to have a winning formula" (Hiestand, 2001); "eToys, whose market capitalization once exceeded that of industry leader Toys 'R' Us Inc., has been selling off its assets piecemeal following its Chapter 11 bankruptcy filing" (Bannon, 2001);
- "Loyal Following Couldn't Keep Jacksonville, Mich.-Based Jacobson's Going" (Wells & Daniels, 2002);
- "Though Americans might not love Krispy Kreme doughnuts as much as the company claimed, the pastries still have legions of loyal fans . . . [Krispy Kreme] is in intensive care, scorned by shareholders, shunned by Wall Street, haunted by investigators and guided by strangers" (Maley, 2005);
- "Garden Botanika, Inc., the Redmond-based cosmetics and personal care products company, announced today it has filed a vol-

untary petition under Chapter 11 of the United States Bankruptcy Code . . . Garden Botanika remains an industry leader with high sales and extremely loyal customers" (*Business Wire,* 1999).

Many would argue that these described scenarios are simply the result of management losing sight of the value that their firms provided customers, or the loss of a bottom-line focus. Perhaps that is true in some cases, but clearly not all. One only need look to the fortunes of an icon of US industry, AT&T, to see that such simple explanations are far from clear-cut and rarely constitute the sole reasons for such results.

For most of the last half of the twentieth century, the name AT&T was synonymous with sophisticated managerial thinking and was frequently cited in the popular business press as a company at the forefront of revolutionary perspectives on management. AT&T advanced the science of customer attitude measurement and management, pioneering the use of customer value analysis (CVA) (Gale, 1994).[1] AT&T demanded that projects meet financial objectives through the use of economic value added (EVA) (Ray, 2001).[2] And AT&T diligently monitored and managed its employees' attitudes to foster a winning environment (Ferling, 1993). To demonstrate its commitment to these objectives, in 1995 the company established the Business Excellence Award, which to win required that a division exceed the industry average in financial performance, customer satisfaction and employee satisfaction (Eisman, 1995). Furthermore, to insure management focus, AT&T's board was regularly supplied with three metrics: customer value, overall quality, and price competitiveness (Sinha & DeSarbo, 1998).

The market of the early twenty-first century, however, buffeted AT&T. It was forced to retreat from its residential business after determining that the majority of the customers it was serving could not be served profitably (Sellend, 2004). Ultimately, AT&T was acquired by SBC Communications, with the combined entity operating under the AT&T banner, to better position the company against its competitors (McKay, 2005; Searcey & Steinberg, 2005).

This is in no way a knock against AT&T. The stumbles of many Malcolm Baldrige Quality Award winners (of which AT&T is one) underscore the fact that "quality" focused companies practicing "advanced" management techniques can and do slip. While there are clearly market factors that uniquely influence the struggles of each firm, when companies find themselves in financial difficulty one thing is almost universally certain: the majority of customers did not produce an acceptable rate of return.

This was certainly true for AT&T's residential business customers, when the company acknowledged and pulled back from this market. A similar reasoning followed the demise of many dotcoms when the bubble burst. Philip J. Kaplan, founder of F**kedcompany.com and author of *F'd Companies*, observed the following regarding the dotcom meltdown: "The thing that is so astounding is just how little can be learned from all of this . . . It's basic business. Buy low and sell high. Don't sell products that you can't make a profit on" (Lorek, 2002).

Philip Kaplan, of course, is undoubtedly correct. The fundamental rule of business is to satisfy customer needs and wants at a profit. Paradoxically, however, a serious concerted effort to truly understand individual customer profitability is really only a decade old. In fact, most firms today still would be hard pressed to say that they have a good understanding of their customers' profitability at the individual level.

This lack of understanding significantly hampers management's ability to make sound customer-focused investment decisions. An examination of individual customer profitability invariably reveals that while organizations will always have some highly profitable customers, they are also likely to have some highly unprofitable customers. Researchers frequently find that the top 20% of customers generate between 150% and 300% of total profits; the middle 60-70% of customers just about break even; and the bottom 10-20% of all customers lose 50% to 200% of total profits (Kaplan & Narayanan, 2001a; Lingle, 1995) (see Figure 1). In essence, the cumulative profitability curve (whale curve) translates to the fact that up to 80% of a typical firm's customers do not provide an acceptable rate of return!

PITFALLS IN POPULAR APPROACHES TO IDENTIFYING "BEST" CUSTOMERS

Given the pareto principle that a relatively small percentage of customers tend to produce all of the profits for a firm, it is imperative that managers know precisely which customers should be targeted for acquisition and retention efforts. Recognition of this fact and attempts to identify best customers are certainly not new. The problem faced by today's marketers is rather that virtually none of the conventional methods does a particularly good job of actually identifying best customers.

FIGURE 1. Cumulative Customer Profitability

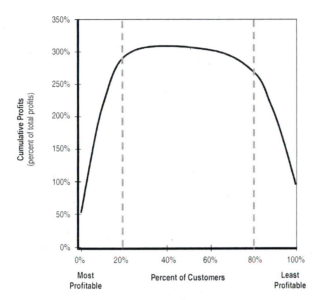

Three of the most common methods that fall into this category are RFM (Recency, Frequency, Monetary Value), Total Revenue, and Contribution to Past Profits.

The RFM Method

RFM has been one of the most widely used methods to identify best customers for the past 30 years–particularly by direct marketers (Hughes, 1996). It is based on the assumption that past purchase behavior can pinpoint a firm's best customers. It uses three main variables in identifying best customers: (1) recency (R), which describes how recently the customer made a purchase; (2) frequency (F), which describes how frequently the customer buys; and finally (3) monetary value (M), which essentially indicates the revenue generated by the customer. The assumption is that the most recent, most frequent, and largest spending customers are the best customers since it is assumed they will act similarly in the future as well. The subsumed belief is that these customers are also probably the most profitable ones.

The stages in a typical RFM analyses include sorting the database in ascending order by these three variables. The database is then divided into quintiles or deciles (depending on how large the database is) for each variable. Each customer is assigned an RFM code that describes where he/she fares in the database relative to other customers.

The popularity of the RFM approach is not surprising given the limited information that is needed to score customers and assign them into groups. Furthermore, most companies keep track of this type of data, making it easily accessible, and no specialized software or sophisticated analyst is needed to conduct the analyses since it is essentially based on a simple indication of quintiles and a subsequent ranking. As a result, RFM methodologies are extremely popular.

There are, however, some serious drawbacks to this approach. First, RFM is primarily a segmentation scheme, assigning customers to a group rather than calculating an individual score for each customer. Second, since it focuses solely on past behavior, it fails to consider future potential or developmental growth (Miglautsch, 2002).

The biggest problem with RFM, however, is that it assumes that how recently, how frequently, and how much a customer spends are the *only* three variables that determine the value of a customer. Clearly, there could be numerous other alternate and/or supplementary factors that determine "best" customers that should be taken into consideration when identifying customers for acquisition or retention efforts.

Total Revenue Approach

The second popular approach to identifying a company's best customers emerged as a result of the inability of firms to gauge profitability easily. This forced most firms to treat customer revenue and customer profitability as highly correlated and even synonymous. Revenue is a measure of purchase volume, and therefore correlated to customer loyalty. As a result, firms tend to expend a great deal of effort on their highest revenue customers. Revenue, however, is typically not a very good predictor of profitability. Some of the largest customers turn out to be the most unprofitable ones.

As a testament to this idea, when examining the chain of effects from share of wallet to revenue and profits, Keiningham, Perkins-Munn, Aksoy, and Estrin (2005) found that the top 25% of financial services customers examined fell either into the top quartile or bottom quartile with regard to their contribution to profits (see Figure 2). Similar findings are discovered for researchers using activity-based cost accounting

FIGURE 2. Example of Relationship Between Customer Revenue and Customer Profitability

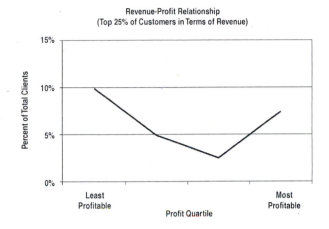

Adapted from Keiningham, Timothy L., Tiffany Perkins-Munn, Lerzan Aksoy, and Demitry Estrin (2005), "Does Customer Satisfaction Lead to Profitability? The Mediating Role of Share-of-Wallet," *Managing Service Quality*, 15 (2), 172-181.

in other industries (Kaplan & Narayanan, 2001b). As Professors Kaplan and Narayanan (2001a) observe: "A company cannot lose large amounts of money with small customers. It doesn't do enough business with a small customer to incur large (absolute) losses. Only a large customer, working in a particularly perverse way can be a large loss customer. Large customers tend to be either the most profitable or the least profitable in the entire customer base. It's unusual for a large customer to be in the middle of the total profitability rankings."

Clearly, there is no substitute for knowing the profitability of customers. While chasing revenue may expand market share, it is definitely not a profit maximizing strategy–at least in the near term.

Contribution to Past Profits Approach

Given that (1) profits are the ultimate measure of success for any firm, (2) customers are the primary assets that generate profits, and (3) most customers do not produce acceptable financial returns, understanding customer profitability has become paramount for managers worldwide. Succinctly defined, customer profitability is the "difference between the revenues earned from and the costs associated with the customer relationship during a specified period" (Pfeifer, Haskins & Conroy, 2005).

For example, a 1998 *Chicago Tribune* article stated, "Customer profitability ratings are something nearly all big banks are working on now, arguing that they must know how much money they can make–or how much they're losing–on individual customers to stay competitive . . . By the end of the year, more than 55 percent of the country's banks plan to be able to calculate customer profitability, according to Gartner Group Mentis Financial Services in Durham, N.C." (Wahl, 1998).

Knowing individual customer profitability has begun to impact corporate strategy. For example, Claudia McElwee, vice president of database marketing and customer information management for CoreStates Bank, reported, "With the high-profit customers, we get the information to the branch [staff] so they can do whatever is necessary to make sure not one leaves the bank. With marginal or break-even customers, we focus on making them more profitable through balance gains and cross-selling. We are especially careful to avoid cross-selling to unprofitable households, but selectively work with a few who show potential. The remainder are divested" (Lingle, 1995).

Additionally, the *Wall Street Journal* reported that Brad Anderson, chief executive officer of Best Buy Co., separate the "angels" (Best Buy's best customers) from its "devils" (its unprofitable customers). "Mr. Anderson says the new tack is based on a business-school theory that advocates rating customers according to profitability, then dumping the up to 20% that are unprofitable" (McWilliams, 2004).

As profits are the life-blood of any company, a focus on customer profitability seems not only intuitive, but the fiduciary responsibility of any corporate officer. Paradoxically, however, a focus on customer profitability is not the best approach to maximizing firm profitability.

Research finds that in order to form an accurate portrayal of not only the current but also the future potential of a customer in terms of profitability, the temporal dimension needs to be incorporated into profitability calculations. As a testament to the importance of a forward-looking perspective, Malthouse and Blattberg (2004) use examples from four industries to demonstrate that a firm cannot assume that high profit customers in the past will be profitable in the future nor can they assume that past low profit customers will remain so in the future as well.

In a four-year study of four U.S. and European companies, representing more than 16,000 individual and corporate customers, Reinartz and Kumar (2002) found that a significant percentage of customers pur-

chase very intensively for a brief period, then never again. They observed that because of their past profitability, one of the companies in
their study had kept this group on its active marketing list for 36 months,
actually transforming these customers into unprofitable customers. This
miscalculation cost the firm about $1 million annually.

LIFETIMES AND LIFETIME VALUES

While the drive to understand customer profitability was clearly a
step in the right direction for companies, it quickly became apparent
that current customer profitability was an insufficient metric for managing alternative investment opportunities. That is because "current" profits are a metric of "past" performance. What is needed, however, is a
forward-looking metric of the stream of profits (or losses) that a customer can be expected to contribute to the firm: in essence, the net present value of a customer's future stream of earnings or customer lifetime
value.

Blattberg and Deighton (1996) were one of the first to suggest the
idea for calculation of what they termed customer equity. They proposed that business growth can occur as a result of acquiring and keeping customers while growing them to their full potential over the
duration of a relationship. In calculating this value, two key components
that need to be accounted for are customer acquisition and retention
costs. The other main elements used are the gross contribution each customer provides and the marketing costs that are incurred for every customer in each time period. In its most basic formulation, the net present
value of these earnings (with probability p in t time periods) produces
the resultant CLV (Dwyer, 1997).

Mainstream marketing has only recently discovered the concepts of
customer lifetimes and lifetime values. Direct marketers originally created these concepts because they required metrics to justify the expense
of finding and keeping customers (Dwyer, 1997; Keane & Wang,
1995). Using a time period or number of identifiable transactions as the
average customer lifetime, direct marketers predict how long a new customer will remain a customer. The concept of customer lifetime also
helps explain why some customers vanish after a certain number of purchase cycles.

Today, customer lifetime value has come to be recognized as one of
the more critical criteria on which customers ought to be evaluated or
scored. As a result, numerous researchers and practitioners have pro-

posed models designed to calculate CLV. For example, Berger and Nasr (1998) present a series of mathematical models for the determination of customer lifetime value that vary in the assumptions they make about the number of sales that take place in the specified time period, the amount of customer retention spending, linearity of profitability and promotion costs, etc. A number of sophisticated mathematical models have also been proposed to advance the precision of CLV calculation (for example, Ching, Ng, Wong & Altman, 2004; Gupta, Lehmann & Stuart, 2004; Jain & Singh, 2002; Kumar, Ramani & Bohling, 2004; Schmittlein & Peterson, 1994; Shih & Liu, 2003). Furthermore, application of CLV has evolved from aggregate measures (entire customer bases, or customer segments) to individual-level calculations (Kumar, Ramani & Bohling, 2004; Libai, Narayandas & Humby, 2002; Venatesan & Kumar, 2004).

Despite the simplicity of the concept, in essence the net present value (NPV) of future earnings, the measurement of CLV demands intense rigor. All cash flows and expenses must be identified and allocated precisely to each customer or type of customer. This approach to handling cost allocations, while familiar to some, is uncharted territory to others. Direct marketers have traditionally assigned the costs of communication, product delivery, and promotions to individual customers (Berger & Nasr-Bechwati, 2001; Dwyer, 1997; Keane & Wang, 1995). On the other hand, for more traditional businesses, firms have the especially daunting task of assigning indirect costs of marketing actions to individual customers or customer segments (Berger et al., 2002). As a solution to this problem, Gurau and Ranchhod (2002) propose following three key costing principles: (1) "customer costs must be related to the revenues they generate"; (2) "not all costs within the organization should be attributed down to a customer level"; (3) "it should be made absolutely clear who can influence different types of cost and revenues."

Despite the difficulties surrounding the calculation of CLV, the rewards for managers make the task well worth the effort. Research has proven CLV to be a superior metric to other traditional, commonly-used measures to identify the most attractive customers, such as RFM and contribution to (current/past) profits (Reinartz & Kumar, 2000). Reasons for the superiority of CLV to other methods of identifying best customers can be summarized as follows:

1. "It is a forward-looking metric, unlike other traditional measures (that include past contribution to profit);

2. It helps marketers to adopt the right marketing activities today to increase future profitability;
3. It is the only metric that incorporates all the elements of revenue, expense, and customer behavior that drive profitability;
4. It enforces the focus on the customer (instead of products) as the driver of profitability" (Keiningham, Vavra, Aksoy, Wallard & Kumar, 2005, p. 204).

USING CLV TO OPTIMIZE PERFORMANCE

Understanding customers' individual lifetime values provides management with critical strategic insight. With this information, managers can set an upper threshold for investing in customer relationships without running the risk of overspending. Simplistically, suppose the CLV for a customer with a high likelihood of defecting is $200 and the firm has a hurdle rate (minimally acceptable return) of 15% on all customers. Then in order to retain the customer, the company can spend approximately $174 (i.e., $200/(1 + 15%) = $173.91) and maintain its desired profitability level.

CLV in and of itself, however, is not a strategy. Rather, it is a financial measure of earnings potential. Hence, this information provides critical information when formulating strategy. Keiningham et al. (2005) propose a five-step process for leveraging CLV data to maximize a firm's future profits (see Figure 3). These steps are identified and discussed below.

Step 1: Observation

This stage consists of accumulating all customers' behavioral data, including:

- purchase records and history,
- costs associated with servicing the customer,
- share of spending (share of wallet) allocation by the customer to the firm and
- demographic data.

Typically, this data emerges from multiple sources within the firm. This presents the challenging task of successful data integration across multiple data sources. This problem occurs mainly because customer

FIGURE 3. A Process for Leveraging CLV to Maximize Profits

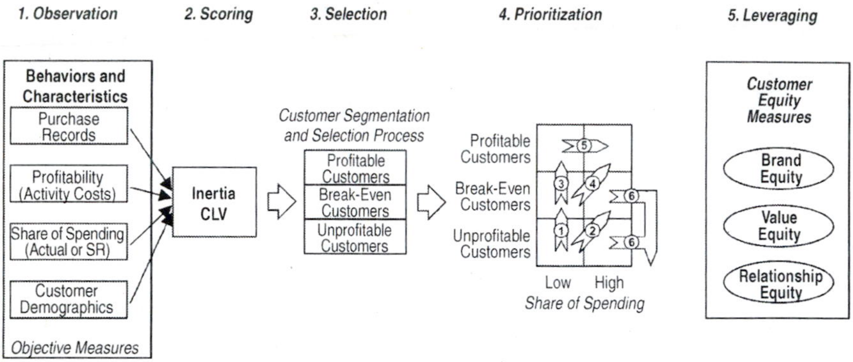

Adapted from: Keiningham, Timothy L., Terry G. Vavra, Lerzan Aksoy, and Henri Wallard (2005), *Loyalty Myths: Hyped Strategies that Will Put You Out of Business and Proven Tactics that Really Work*. Hoboken, NJ: John Wiley and Sons.

data is frequently stored in databases with conflicting architectures, differing content, and inconsistent data formats. Therefore, the first stage prior to any data analysis is ensuring data validity, reliability and accuracy by creating a database merged at the individual customer level through the use of a uniform "key" (customer identifier) existing in all databases.

Step 2: Scoring

Based on the observed behavioral data collected in stage 1, it becomes possible to calculate an "inertial" lifetime value for each customer. Inertial lifetime value represents the expected CLV of each customer were the firm to take no action. This baseline CLV calculation can then be used as an intermediate step for classification purposes in the next step; it does not imply that this is the best CLV for each customer.

Step 3: Selection

Using the inertial CLV calculated for each customer, customers can be allocated to one of the three customer types based upon their future profitability to the firm: Profitable Customers, Break-Even Customers, and Unprofitable Customers. While the allocation is seemingly obvious, the message from this step is probably quite profound. The proportion of customers in each category reveals how well the company has managed its customer relationships and provides a strong indication as to the overall financial health of the firm. More importantly, the resulting segments become the foundation of a truly effective customer loyalty initiative.

Step 4: Prioritization

After classification of customers based upon their value to the firm has been completed, an additional segmentation based on their current share of spending is proposed. This share-of-spending metric enables each customer to be categorized into either the low share or high share-of-spending category. Hence, with the help of the "customer value/share-of-spending" matrix, all customers can be classified into one of six cells. These carry with it unique implementation strategies that can be summarized as follows:

Suggested Strategies for Unprofitable/Low Share Customers:

- Migrating unprofitable low share customers to the status of break-even low share customers (strategy 1).
- Migrating unprofitable low share customers to break-even high share customers (strategy 2).
- Divesting unprofitable low share customers whose status cannot be improved (strategy 6).

Suggested Strategies for Break-Even/Low Share Customers:

- Migrating break-even low share customers to profitable low share customers (strategy 3).
- Migrating break-even low share customers to profitable high share customers (strategy 4).
- Divesting break-even low share customers whose status cannot be improved (strategy 6).

Suggested Strategies for Profitable/Low Share Customers:

- Migrating profitable low share customers to profitable high share customers (strategy 5).

Each of these strategies can be tested by computing its corresponding ROI, allowing the firm to select the opportunity that represents the best investment decision.

Step 5: Leveraging

Each strategy requires moving as many customers as possible from one condition to another. To be able to accomplish this task, there are several sources of customer equity that managers can influence. Rust, Zeithaml and Lemon (2000, 2004) define the construct of customer equity by incorporating both brand-centric and customer-centric marketing activities. Customer equity includes:

1. Value Equity–the customer's objective assessment of the utility of a brand. This assessment is driven by the product's quality, price and convenience.
2. Brand Equity–the customer's subjective and intangible assessment of the brand built through image and meaning. This assessment is influenced by brand awareness, the consumer's attitude toward the brand, and the firm's corporate citizenship.
3. Relationship Equity–a subjective predisposition to stay with a brand because of its familiarity, difficulties of switching, or a trust in the brand's sales staff.

The components of customer equity are in essence proposed to be the key drivers of a firm's efforts to improve customers' CLV. They provide an action component for each strategy: how to leverage aspects of the customer and brand experience to grow customers in the way that is desired. In other words, they are levers to migrate customers using one or more of the six implementation strategies.

Prioritization among the customer equity components can be made based on the ROI calculated for each component. An assumed "take" (probability of migration on the part of customers) will have to be used to calculate the impact on greater spending and consequently an improved CLV. The three components of customer equity can then be rank-ordered according to the potential impact from improvements on each.

CONCLUSION

Customers are the preeminent assets of any firm: the source of all profits. Unfortunately, most of a firm's customers do not produce an acceptable rate of return. Therefore, knowing which customers represent the best assets to the firm is critical to effective strategy development, and ultimately to maximizing profitability.

Customer lifetime value analysis provides the critical metric for correctly identifying a company's best customers. As such, CLV provides managers with the requisite information to ensure that their efforts to attract and retain customers pay real dividends.

It is important to recognize that the methods for calculating CLV will continue to evolve (becoming ever more precise). But the current state of CLV analysis offers managers an unprecedented opportunity to fulfill the fundamental goal of all businesses: to satisfy customer needs and wants at a profit. By understanding customers' potential lifetime value, firms can nurture profitable, long-term relationships with customers by providing them with the level of service that they truly believe is worth what they are willing to pay.

NOTES

1. It should be noted that despite the name, Customer Value Analysis (CVA) focuses on aggregate customer measures perceptions rather than individual customer/client profitability, using ratios of aggregate performance perceptions for a firm and its competitors.

2. In a 1993 cover story, *Fortune* magazine called EVA "today's hottest financial idea and getting hotter" (Tully, 1993).

REFERENCES

Bannon, L. (2001). Out-of-business eToys sells its web site, trademark and other assets to KB toys. *Wall Street Journal* (May 18), B8.

Berger, P. D., Bolton, R. N., Bowman, D., Briggs, E., Kumar, V., Parasuraman, A. & Terry, C. (2002). Marketing actions and the value of customer assets: A framework for customer asset management. *Journal of Service Research, 5,* 1 (August), 69-76.

Berger, P. D. & Nasr, N. I. (1998). Customer lifetime value: Marketing models and applications. *Journal of Interactive Marketing, 12* (Winter), 17-30.

Berger, P. D. & Nasr, N. I. (2001). The allocation of promotion budget to maximize customer equity. *OMEGA, 29,* 49-61.

Blattberg, R. C. & Deighton, J. (1996). Manage market by the customer equity test. *Harvard Business Review, 73,* 136-144.

Blattberg, R. C., Getz, G. & Thomas, J. S. (2001). *Customer equity: Building and managing relationships as valuable assets.* Boston: Harvard Business School Press.

Anonymour (1999). Garden botanika makes chapter 11 bankruptcy filing with $7.0 million in debtor-in-possession financing; Store closings to be a part of reorganization effort. *Business Wire* (April 20).

Ching, W-K, Ng, M. K., Wong, K. K. & Altman, E. (2004). Customer lifetime value: Stochastic optimization approach. *Journal of the Operational Research Society, 55,* 860-868.

Dwyer, R. (1997). Customer lifetime valuation to support marketing decision making. *Journal of Direct Marketing, 3* (4), 8-15.

Eisman, R. (1995). Eyes on the prize. *Incentive, 169,* 1 (January), 43-47.

Ferling, R. L. (1993). Quality in 3D: EVA, CVA, and employees. *Financial Executive, 9,* 4 (July/August), 51.

Gale, B. (1994). *Managing customer value: Creating quality and service that customers can see.* New York, NY: The Free Press.

Gupta, S. & Lehmann, D. R. (2005). *Managing customers as investments: The strategic value of customers in the long run.* Upper Saddle River, NJ: Wharton School Publishing.

Gupta, S., Lehmann, D. R. & Stuart, J. A. (2004), Valuing customers. *Journal of Marketing Research, 41,* 1 (February), 7-18.

Gurau, C. & Ranchhod, A. (2002). How to calculate the value of a customer—Measuring customer satisfaction: A platform for calculating, predicting and increasing customer profitability. *Journal of Targeting, Measurement and Analysis for Marketing, 10,* no. 3 (March), 203-219.

Hiestand, J. (2001). Is eToys winding down? Poor sales hurting cash-strapped company. *Daily News* (Los Angeles, CA) (January 27), B1.

Hughes, A. (1996). Boosting response with RFM. *American Demographics,* 4-10.

Jain, D. & Singh, S. S. (2002). Customer lifetime value research in marketing: A review and future directions. *Journal of Interactive Marketing, 16,* 2 (Spring), 34-46.

Kaplan, R. S. & Narayanan, V. G. (2001)a. *Customer profitability measurement and management.* White Paper (May), Acorn Systems, Inc.: Houston, TX. <http://www.acornsys.com/value/whitepapers/WP-CustomerProfitabilityMM.html>.

Kaplan, R. S. & Narayanan, V. G. (2001)b. Measuring and managing customer profitability. *Cost Management, 15,* no. 5 (September/October), 5-15.

Keane, T. & Wang, P. (1995). Applications for the lifetime value model in modern newspaper publishing. *Journal of Direct Marketing, 9* (2), 59-66.

Keiningham, T. L., Perkins-Munn, T., Aksoy, L. & Estrin, D. (2005). Does customer satisfaction lead to profitability? The mediating role of share-of-wallet. *Managing Service Quality, 15* (2), 172-181.

Keiningham, T. L., Vavra, T. G., Aksoy, L., Wallard, H. & Kumar, V. (2005). The right way to manage for customer loyalty, in *Loyalty myths: Hyped strategies that will put you out of business and proven tactics that really work,* by Keiningham, Vavra, Aksoy, and Wallard, Hoboken, NJ: John Wiley and Sons.

Kumar, V., Ramani, G. & Bohling, T. (2004). Customer lifetime value approaches and best practice applications. *Journal of Interactive Marketing, 18,* 3 (Summer), 60-72.

Libai, B., Narayandas, D. & Humby, C. (2002). Toward an individual customer profitability model: A segment-based approach. *Journal of Service Research, 5,* no. 1 (August), 69-76.

Lingle, S. (1995). How much is a customer worth? *Bank Marketing, 27,* 8 (August), 13-16.

Lorek, L. A. (2002). Ten worst dot-coms show how bad ideas fed the web bust. *Knight Ridder Tribune Business News* (May 18), 1.

Maley, F. (2005). Glazed and confused. *Business North Carolina* (August), 36-44.

Malthouse, E. C. & Blattberg, R. C. (2004). Can we predict customer lifetime value. *Journal of Interactive Marketing, 19* (1).

McKay, M. (2005). SBC sees buyout of AT&T as rescue. *Knight Ridder Tribune Business News* (February 1), 1.

McWilliams, G. (2004). Minding the store: Analyzing customers, Best Buy decides not all are welcome. *Wall Street Journal* (November 8), A1.

Miglautsch, J. R. (2002). Application of R-F-M principles: What to do with 1-1-1 customers? *Journal of Database Marketing, 9,* 319-324.

Niraj, R., Gupta, M. & Narasimhan, C. (2001). Customer profitability in a supply chain. *Journal of Marketing, 65* (July), 1-16.

Pfeifer, P. E., Haskins, M. E. & Conroy, R. E. (2005). Customer lifetime value, customer profitability, and the treatment of acquisition spending. *Journal of Managerial Issues, 17,* no. 1 (Spring), 11-25.

Ray, R. (2001). Economic value added: Theory, evidence, a missing link. *Review of Business, 22,* 1/2 (Spring), 66-70.

Reinartz, W. J. & Kumar, V. (2000). On the profitability of long-life customers in a noncontractual setting: An empirical investigation and implications for marketing. *Journal of Marketing, 64* (4), 17-35.

Reinartz, W. J. & Kumar, V. (2002). The mismanagement of customer loyalty. *Harvard Business Review* (July), 86-94.

Rust, R. T., Zeithaml, V. A. & Lemon, K. N. (2000). *Driving customer equity: How customer lifetime value is reshaping corporate strategy.* New York: The Free Press.

Rust, R. T., Zeithaml, V. A. & Lemon, K. N. (2004). Customer-centered brand management. *Harvard Business Review, 82* (9), 110-118.

Schmittlein, D. C. & Peterson, R. A. (1994). Customer base analysis: An industrial purchase application. *Marketing Science, 13,* 41-67.

Schumpeter, J. A. (1942). *Capitalism, socialism and democracy.* New York: Harper & Brothers.

Searcey, D. & Steinberg, B. (2005). SBC's embrace of AT&T brand brings history–and baggage. *The Wall Street Journal* (October 28), B1.

Sellend, C. (2004). You're fired! *Customer Relationship Management, 8,* no. 10 (October), 24.

Shallit, B. (2002). Broke but beloved. Bob Shallit Column, *The Sacramento Bee* (May 27), D1.

Shih, Y-Y & Liu, C-Y (2003). A method for customer lifetime value ranking–Combining the analytic hierarchy process and clustering analysis. *Database Marketing & Customer Strategy Management, 11* (2), 159-172.

Sinha, I. & DeSarbo, W. S. (1998). An integrated approach toward the spatial modeling of perceived customer value. *Journal of Marketing Research, 32* (2), 236-249.

Tully, S. (1993). The real key to creating wealth. *Fortune, 128,* 6 (September 20), 38-52.

Venatesan, R. & Kumar, V. (2004). A customer lifetime value framework for customer selection and resource allocation strategy. *Journal of Marketing, 68,* 4, 106-125.

Wahl, M. (1998). Sizing up customers: Are you happy with your bank? More and more that may depend on how happy your bank is with you. *Chicago Tribune* (November 8), 1.
Wells, J. & Daniels, E. (2002). Loyal following couldn't keep Jacksonville, Mich.-based Jacobson's going. *The Florida Times-Union* (July 27). <http://www.jacksonville.com/tu-online/stories/072702/bus_10025835.html>

doi:10.1300/J366v05n02_03

Customer Lifetime Value as the Basis of Customer Segmentation: Issues and Challenges

Katherine N. Lemon

Boston College

Tanya Mark

University of Western Ontario

SUMMARY. In this article, we examine current trends in customer lifetime value and customer segmentation models and identify key issues for future research. CLV-based segmentation is a segmentation approach that groups customers into meaningful segments based upon customer lifetime value and (potentially) other factors. In the article, we discuss the extent to which CLV-based segmentation meets the criteria

Katherine N. Lemon, PhD, is Associate Professor of Marketing, Wallace E. Carroll School of Management, Boston College, Fulton Hall, 140 Commonwealth Avenue, Chestnut Hill, MA 02467 (E-mail: katherine.lemon@bc.edu).

Tanya Mark is a PhD candidate, Richard Ivey School of Business, University of Western Ontario, 1151 Richmond Street N., London, Ontario, N6A 3K7 (E-mail: tmark@ivey.uwo.ca).

The authors are listed in alphabetical order and contributed equally to the manuscript.

[Haworth co-indexing entry note]: "Customer Lifetime Value as the Basis of Customer Segmentation: Issues and Challenges." Lemon, Katherine N., and Tanya Mark. Co-published simultaneously in *Journal of Relationship Marketing* (Best Business Books, an imprint of The Haworth Press, Inc.) Vol. 5, No. 2/3, 2006, pp. 55-69; and: *Customer Lifetime Value: Reshaping the Way We Manage to Maximize Profits* (ed: David Bejou, Timothy L. Keiningham, and Lerzan Aksoy) Best Business Books, an imprint of The Haworth Press, Inc., 2006, pp. 55-69. Single or multiple copies of this article are available for a fee from The Haworth Document Delivery Service [1-800-HAWORTH, 9:00 a.m. - 5:00 p.m. (EST). E-mail address: docdelivery@haworthpress.com].

for effective segmentation. We also identify six areas for future research: (1) models and management of "micro-segments," (2) using CLV-based segmentation to improve the efficiency of marketing programs, (3) the need for more dynamic CLV-based segmentation models, (4) applying CLV-based customer segmentation to new products and new customers, (5) challenges associated with implementing CLV-based segmentation, and (6) the need for new models that enable firms to segment customers by response to marketing activities and CLV at different points in the customer decision process. doi:10.1300/J366v05n02_04 *[Article copies available for a fee from The Haworth Document Delivery Service: 1-800-HAWORTH. E-mail address: <docdelivery@haworthpress. com> Website: <http://www.HaworthPress.com> © 2006 by The Haworth Press, Inc. All rights reserved.]*

KEYWORDS. Customer lifetime value, customer segmentation, customer equity

INTRODUCTION

Why do firms employ customer segmentation and customer lifetime value (CLV) models? In a perfect world, using these models would allow firms to tailor their products to specific customers, and then select appropriate marketing actions that maximize customer response. In addition, in such a perfect world, we would be able to improve the efficiency and effectiveness of these marketing approaches and, when possible, reduce marketing expenditures so as to maximize firms' overall profitability. However, as such perfection is difficult to achieve, these objectives, collectively, represent an overwhelming challenge. In this article, we examine the contribution that emerging models of CLV-based customer segmentation models and approaches can make to these daunting goals and set forth an agenda for future research in this area.

Why is segmentation important and how is it changing?

Segmentation is a fundamental strategy to managing marketing efforts directed at customers. It was introduced in the 1950s to reflect a change from mass marketing to the new (at that time) marketing concept: targeting products and/or marketing campaigns to specific groups of customers. CLV is changing segmentation because of the increased pressure to view each and every customer as an asset (Rust, Lemon, and Zeithaml, 2004). Further, incorporating customer profitability into segmentation strategies enables an organization to improve the effectiveness and efficiency of their marketing programs (Niraj, Gupta, and Narasimhan, 2001).

According to a recent article by Forrester Research (Kolko and Gazala, 2005), firms are experiencing increased pressure to offer customer-centric strategies because many of their competitors are offering one-to-one or customized marketing strategies. Customers' expectations are changing, and as a result, companies need to better understand customer needs, preferences, and profitability in order to better acquire new customers, and better serve and retain their current customers. With advances in technology and segmentation methods, segmentation strategies are evolving to reflect this shift in power toward the customer.

Today, managers have access to an abundance of data about their customers, including their purchasing history, attitudinal data collected from customer satisfaction surveys, and demographic and socioeconomic data collected from rewards/loyalty programs. Segmentation offers managers one approach to utilize these data to customize the firm's marketing efforts, but successful segmentation efforts require sophisticated models to use relevant information, and to most effectively target specific customers with appropriate offers to maximize response. In addition, recent research and cost/benefit analysis suggests that, in some industries, a CLV-segmentation strategy, i.e., clustering customers into meaningful segments based upon customer profitability and other variables, may be a more appropriate use of a firm's resources than individual-level customer profitability models (Libai, Narayandas, and Humby, 2002). There are several factors that may contribute to the difficulties and high costs of developing and implementing CLV-based segmentation strategies: software requirements, employee incentives, human resources needed to understand individual needs and preferences, customized firm-level modeling requirements, and the difficulties associated with transforming these demands into targeted marketing campaigns and new products and services.

CLV and customer profitability are fast becoming accepted as new bases to customer segmentation. Firms are building on (or in some cases replacing) traditional bases of segmentation such as geographic, demographic, socioeconomic, attitudinal, and behavioral to incorporate customer past and projected purchase data into customer segmentation models, customer portfolio models and resource allocation decision-making (Johnson and Selnes 2004, 2005). These models provide sales and account managers another lens through which to understand and prioritize their customers, and to evaluate the efficiency and effectiveness of their marketing and sales programs and resource allocations.

What is CLV-based customer segmentation?

In this article, we define CLV-based segmentation as a segmentation approach used by a firm that groups customers into meaningful segments based upon customer lifetime value and potentially other factors. Typically, this process involves some variant of the following steps:

1. Gather data to analyze the current and potential profitability of current customers.
2. Develop a firm-specific model for calculating customer lifetime value, defined as the sum of accumulated cash flows of a customer (in terms of profit) over the customer's lifetime with the company, discounted to the present.
3. Categorize customers based upon their customer lifetime value, and utilize these groups, potentially along with other factors, as the segmentation structure.
4. Develop distinct marketing approaches for each segment, allocating additional resources to those segments with high CLV, and fewer resources to those segments with low or negative CLV.

How does CLV change the objective of segmentation models?

Segmentation is not a natural phenomenon–it is a managerially imposed market structure employed to improve the effectiveness and efficiency of marketing strategies (e.g., product development, positioning, advertising, pricing) and tactical decisions (customer acquisition and retention, resource allocation decisions, how much, to whom, and when). There is no one perfect approach to segmenting a market; the best segmentation model is the one that (a) provides insight to managers regarding current and potential customers, and (b) enables managers to effectively reach the market and gain appropriate customer response. Traditionally, objectives of segmentation strategies focused on identifying groups of potential customers, e.g., profiling prospects for product development, identifying appropriate prospects for marketing campaigns, and classifying groups in accordance with their potential response to specific pricing strategies. However, incorporating customer profitability measures such as CLV into segmentation approaches changes these objectives. CLV enables a firm to focus on improving the effectiveness of marketing expenditures. For example, using CLV as a basis, a segmentation objective may focus on evaluating customer migration expenditures. Libai et al. (2002) define migration expenditures as all marketing activities aimed at improving the profitability level of customers and at reducing the number of customers that become less profitable over time. Similarly, the firm's objective may be to identify segments of potential customers with high CLV. Kumar, Venkatesan and Reinarz (2006) suggest such an application of CLV-based segmentation and show how it can improve market resource allocation (see also Venkatesan and Kumar 2004; Rust, Zeithaml, and Lemon, 2000).

HOW DOES CLV COMPLICATE SEGMENTATION STRATEGIES?

It is useful to examine how customer lifetime value may influence the effectiveness of segmentation strategies. Wedel and Kamakura (1998) identified several criteria for effective segmentation: identifiability, substantiality, accessibility, stability, actionability and responsiveness. Below, we identify potential complicating issues brought on by customer lifetime value-based segmentation utilizing these six criteria.

- *Identifiability*: Can homogenous segments be identified? It may be difficult for firms to capture, track, and merge the necessary data to calculate CLV. In addition, there are many measures and approaches to calculating CLV, and the decision of which approach to use may hinder attempts to identify distinct segments.
- *Substantiality*: Are segments large enough to justify marketing resource allocations? Typically, CLV is calculated at the individual customer level, for existing customers of a firm. However, individual-level CLV may not be appropriate for all industries, particularly some consumer markets. Thus it is important to consider the costs and benefits associated with individual versus some broader cluster or segment analysis of CLV, and to determine the situations in which individual or segment-level is more appropriate. Finally, market size and market structure may also influence the substantiality of a CLV-based segmentation approach.
- *Accessibility*: Will promotions targeted at segments reach the intended audience? Typically, CLV-based segmentation approaches seek to identify the current or potentially most valuable customers,

and to target them with marketing actions. However, we are just beginning to scratch the surface in terms of understanding how CLV can enhance our ability to target customers. For example, Reinartz, Thomas, and Kumar (2005) show that CLV models can identify which customers to target with what type of marketing communication at what point in time, and can enable firms to allocate limited resources to the most valuable (or most promising) customers. This area of research is promising and suggests that incorporating CLV into traditional segmentation strategies can improve the effectiveness (and perhaps efficiency) of marketing campaigns.

- *Stability*: Does the segment membership or segment profile change over time? It is necessary for a segment to remain stable for a long enough duration to build a profile of the segment, identify a strategic approach, implement the approach and evaluate the success of a campaign. This issue has not yet received rigorous attention in the literature (Wedel and Kamakura, 1998; Steenkamp and Ter Hofstede, 2002). Static segmentation models make the implicit assumption of stability; however, from a managerial perspective, the stability of a segment's characteristics and membership structure over time is important because it would otherwise make the model ineffective at meeting its objectives. Also, if a segment's size or characteristics change over time, then a small segment size may be insufficient justification to warrant a target marketing strategy for specific segments. Finally, because of the inherent assumptions and data requirements necessary to calculate CLV, the stability of segments may change over time. This suggests a need for dynamic CLV-based segmentation models as, although these models (by design) are not necessarily stable, they are likely to be more accurate than static models in terms of predicting customer profitability.

- *Actionability*: Does the segmentation approach result in effective targeted marketing efforts? It is important to consider how CLV as a basis may improve the effectiveness of a targeted marketing campaign. Recent research suggests that CLV enables managers to improve the allocation of marketing resources to the most valuable customers (Reinartz, Thomas, and Kumar, 2005). However, it is not clear that CLV, per se, improves the actual *effectiveness* of a given marketing campaign. Rather, it is a matter of determining which strategy may be more effective in changing customers' buying patterns based on their profitability levels (e.g., can a given campaign reduce service costs for less profitable customers, or increase cross-buying of more profitable products or services for current customers?).

- *Responsiveness*: Do the segments respond uniquely to marketing efforts targeted toward them? The issue here is one of understanding how managers should allocate resources (which strategy is more effective/efficient) to each segment based on the segment's CLV or customer profitability. If a segment is not responsive to marketing efforts but highly profitable, then it may be in the best interest of the firm to allocate resources to determine why the segment is not responding. On the other hand, if the segment is not responsive and not profitable, then the firm may decide not to do anything, or to "terminate" the relationship with these customers.

Overall, the above discussion suggests that incorporating CLV into customer segmentation models may be challenging, but may also be significantly financially rewarding. CLV-based segmentation, if done well, appears to meet the criteria of identifiability, accessibility and (potentially) substantiality, and actionability. However, the resulting segments may not be stable, and may not differ uniquely in terms of responsiveness.

ISSUES FOR FUTURE RESEARCH: IMPLICATIONS OF CLV AND SEGMENTATION STRATEGY

As firms continue to improve in their abilities to track and calculate customer lifetime value, there are several issues that need to be better understood. Below, we discuss six areas that are ripe for future research. First, CLV-based segmentation suggests that it may be efficient to develop and manage smaller "micro-segments." Second, incorporating CLV into segmentation approaches suggests that we should be able to improve efficiency of marketing programs. Third, we see a need for more dynamic CLV-based segmentation models, highlighting the importance of understanding how marketing resource allocations affect the profitability of customers over time. Fourth, most current CLV models focus on existing customers of the firm for existing products marketed by the firm. New research is needed to apply CLV-based customer segmentation to new products and new customers. Fifth, there are significant challenges associated with implementing CLV-based segmentation. Finally, we believe there is a need for new models that enable firms to segment customers by customer response to marketing activities and CLV at different points in the customer decision process.

Smaller Micro-Segments

Customers may have similar profiles, but different profitability levels. For example, two customers may have similar satisfaction levels, similar age profiles, similar buying history with the firm, yet different profitability levels (perhaps due to channel choices or costs-to-serve). This pattern can occur, for example, when a firm has multiple customers who seek the same features in a product or service, but who differ in terms of service expectations. Therefore, some customers may cost more to serve over the lifetime of the relationship. By incorporating profitability into the segmentation model, the existing profile can be further divided into profitable and less profitable segments, and managers can decide how to allocate resources accordingly.

It is not clear, however, how thinly these segments should be "sliced" in terms of CLV. Libai et al. (2002) suggest that, in frequently packaged consumer goods markets, the benefit of individual level customer profitability models relative to the costs may not be substantial to warrant individual-level analysis but that broader CLV-based segments may do better. However, in business-to-business and direct marketing settings, individual analysis may be more appropriate. This suggests that future research should examine the extent to which micro-segments or "segments of one" can meet the criteria for successful segmentation set out by Wedel and Kamakura (1998), and the specific contexts in which individual models versus cluster or segment-based models are more appropriate.

Improve Efficiency of Marketing Programs

Much research in the area of customer lifetime value has focused on the extent to which customer lifetime value modeling can improve the efficiency of marketing programs (Venkatesan and Kumar, 2004; Reinartz, Thomas, and Kumar, 2005; Rust, Lemon, and Zeithaml, 2004; Zeithaml, Rust, and Lemon, 2001). Broadly, this approach is straightforward: allocate more resources to those current and future customers who are more valuable. Much of this research has implied an underlying segmentation structure based upon customer lifetime value. For example, Zeithaml, Rust, and Lemon (2001) suggest dividing customers into tiers, using CLV as a metric, from "gold" to "lead" and designing service and marketing programs for each tier. However, additional research is needed to link the significant amount of research and knowledge built up in the area of segmentation (e.g., our understanding of the role of heterogeneity and the value of latent-class models) and CLV approaches.

Dynamic Segmentation Models

A critical area for future research is the development of dynamic CLV-based customer segmentation models. It is important to understand how marketing resource allocations affect the profitability of customers over time. Recent research has begun to examine this issue, seeking to understand what to market, to whom, at what point in time (e.g., Venkatesan and Kumar, 2004; Reinartz, Thomas, and Kumar, 2005; Thomas and Sullivan, 2005). However, given that customers develop and change their response behavior over time, segment membership may not be stable over time. Therefore, dynamic models are required that specifically model the migration of customers from less profitable to more profitable segments (or vice versa). Specific challenges that can be addressed as these dynamic models are developed are: (a) understanding and modeling the factors that may influence customer migration from one CLV-segment to another, (b) modeling the process by which customers change and update their response behavior, and (c) determining how to forecast customer changes in tastes, trends and behavior (Zeithaml et al. 2006).

Models for New Products and New Customers

As we consider the link between customer lifetime value and customer segmentation, it is also useful to consider how CLV approaches can improve segmentation decisions for introducing new products and attracting new customers. For example, Hogan, Lemon, and Libai (2002) show that customers who stop using a service (customers who "disadopt") early in the diffusion process are more costly to the firm in terms of future profits than customers (with the same CLV) who disadopt later in the diffusion process. Additional research is needed to determine whether CLV models can also inform our understanding of overall market potential, which customers or segments to target with new products or services, or even the entire new product development process.

As most CLV models to date have focused on current or existing customers (see Rust, Lemon, and Zeithaml, 2004, for a model that also incorporates customer switching from competitors), additional research is also needed to understand how CLV approaches can inform firms' decisions of what *potential* customers to target. Harrah's Entertainment is moving toward this approach with its opportunistic customer segmentation strategies (Lal and Carrolo, 2002). Utilizing only information gained on a customer's first visit to the casino, Harrah's has developed proprietary models to forecast the customer's future potential, thereby determining in advance what offers are most appropriate for that customer.

Facing Implementation Challenges

As firms seek to implement CLV-based segmentation approaches, there are four key areas that present challenges: data and analysis, strategy development, program implementation, and evaluation. As the field of customer management begins to mature, we need to enhance our understanding of what is necessary to successfully develop and implement these approaches.

First, collecting the right data and developing analytic tools is critical. This is, perhaps, the area in which the field of customer management is furthest along. It is understood, for example, that firms need sufficient data and analysis to determine: (a) who the current and potential customers (or customer segments) are, (b) the CLVs of each current and potential customer (or segments), and (c), the drivers of behavior for current and potential customers. In addition, these analyses need to be available throughout the organization, at appropriate levels (e.g., across customer groups, or across geographic regions). Additional research is needed to enhance our understanding of the following:

- What information needs to be collected and by whom?
- What role in the organization should analyze the data?
- What is the role of IT in data collection and analytics?
- What is flow of data in the organization and does it support customer growth?
- What are the appropriate analyses?

Second, developing strategies that utilize the key insights from the analyses is also challenging. The organization needs to be structured to enable a 360° view of customers for each customer group. Successful strategy depends upon (a) having a culture that supports investment in customer initiatives, (b) a CLV-based process for customer segmentation and selection, and (c) a focus on customers–not products, i.e., an understanding of key drivers of customer behavior and how they link to firm capabilities. Future research in this area could examine the ways in which an organization's structure, culture and goals may support or impede strategic customer opportunities.

Third, the actual implementation of specific marketing programs utilizing CLV-based customer segmentation poses its own additional challenges. Sufficient budget and staffing must be allocated for each initiative, and it must often be implemented across geographic regions (often with distinct language, cultural or other barriers). In addition, successful implementation requires an integrated marketing approach to customers (including integrated marketing communications, and pricing consistent with customer expectations), and must often be implemented through and in cooperation with the distribution channel. Future research should examine best practices in the implementation of these strategies, and identify key bottlenecks in the process.

Drilling Down: Drivers of CLV Throughout the Decision Process

Considering the recent advances in our understanding of CLV-based segmentation, we propose that a critical area for future research is the development of dynamic models that incorporate customer segmentation and CLV into the overall consumer decision process. We believe that the next step in the development of CLV-based segmentation approaches will be models that will enable firms to segment customers by customer response to marketing activities and customer CLV at *different points* in the customer decision process. What is now needed is a set of models that enable firms to segment customers throughout the decision process, understanding (a) how customers respond to distinct marketing activities at each point in the decision process, (b) how these customer responses then influence the customer's lifetime value, and (c) which customers (or customer segments, newly defined in this way) the firm should focus on to maximize long-term profitability.

Consider that customers go through a decision process in order to purchase or to repurchase a product or service. Firms traditionally have segmented customers prior to purchase, to determine which customers (or segments) to target with their offerings. However, the advent of customer metrics such as CLV has enabled firms also to segment their customers after initial purchase, based upon potential customer value. Thus, currently we have developed models that enable firms to understand the key drivers of CLV and customer equity. In addition, we have developed sophisticated segmentation models that enable firms to understand how different customers respond differently to marketing actions (consider latent class models such as Kamakura, Kim, and Lee, 1996). Third, we have developed models that examine the relationships among various aspects of the customer consideration and purchase process (e.g., Mittal and Kamakura, 2001; Rust and Verhoef, 2005). However, what is now needed is to bring these elements together in a CLV-based segmentation approach that also takes into account the fact that customers may respond differently at various points in the purchase process.

Such an approach would recognize that firms engage in marketing actions, throughout the consumer decision process, to move consumers to the next stage of the process. CLV and customer segmentation models could be used to determine who, based upon the nature of responses in moving consumers from one stage in the process (say awareness) to a more advanced stage (say consideration), is most likely to become a high CLV customer or customer segment. These "high-potential" consumers become the top-tier candidates for marketing actions designed to move customers from consideration to purchase and beyond. The key distinction here is that consumers may follow *different paths* through the decision process that lead to high CLV. Some highly valuable customers, for example, may move directly from awareness to purchase, and may require little marketing intervention or actions. Other valuable customers may require much more hand-holding throughout the purchase process, but may be much more profitable in the long run.

It is important to identify the most important drivers for each customer segment at *each decision stage*–to maximize customer lifetime value. Such a model would incorporate customer response-based measurement models at each step of the consumer/customer decision process. In addition, it would link marketing actions to CLV throughout the customer decision process, from initial awareness to purchase, repurchase and cross-buying (Bolton, Lemon, and Verhoef, 2004). Finally, it would be able to segment customers by customer response to marketing actions and CLV throughout the customer decision-making process.

Why would this be valuable? This type of model, or set of models, would have many distinct advantages over our current models. First, customer knowledge is captured at all steps of the decision process, and is linked to customer lifetime value. Second, marketing actions become targeted, customized, measurable, and accountable, at every step in the decision process. Third, marketing expenditures can become even more efficient as customers who are unlikely to migrate to purchase (or repurchase) are no longer targeted, or are targeted with less expensive marketing activities. Fourth, such models may enable marketing and sales teams to work more closely together to focus on long-term growth. Finally, the result should be higher CLV per customer and lower marketing costs overall.

Clearly, we are calling for a complex, dynamic decision calculus that combines current approaches to CLV-based customer segmentation with current models of consumer behavior and decision-making. We recognize that this will be a challenge to develop and will require researchers from diverse fields to work together. However, we hope that future research will move in this direction, eventually leading to models that can enable firms to realize the full benefits of CLV-based customer segmentation.

CONCLUSIONS

This article was motivated by our discussions with companies about the challenges of implementing customer lifetime value and customer equity models. Over the past few years, it has become clear to us that there is a reawakening of interest in customer segmentation. Consider, for example, Kumar, Venkatesan and Reinartz's (2006) article, "Knowing What to Sell, When, and to Whom." This article highlights the critical advances that have been made in the last several years linking customer lifetime value, customer segmentation and marketing actions. In addition, there have been some significant advances in our ability to model customer segmentation and heterogeneity over the past decade. Thus, in this article, we have tried to outline a new agenda for customer segmentation–linking it more directly to customer behaviors and customer lifetime value. We believe that there is a significant opportunity for future research on this topic, and we look forward to seeing continued (and accelerated) advances to the field of CLV-based customer segmentation in the next few years.

REFERENCES

Bolton, R., K. Lemon and P. Verhoef (2004). "The Theoretical Underpinnings of Customer Asset Management: A Framework and Propositions for Future Research." *Journal of Academy of Marketing Science* 32(3): 271-292.

Hogan, J., K. Lemon and B. Libai (2003). "What Is the True Value of a Lost Customer?" *Journal of Service Research* 5 (February), 196-208.

Hogan, J., K. Lemon and R. Rust (2002). "Customer Equity Management: Charting New Directions for the Future of Marketing." *Journal of Service Research* 5(1): 4-12.

Johnson, M. and F. Selnes (2004). "Customer Portfolio Management: Toward a Dynamic Theory of Exchange Relationships." *Journal of Marketing* 68(2): 1-17.

Johnson, M. and F. Selnes (2005). "Diversifying Your Customer Portfolio." *MIT Sloan Management Review* 46(3): 11-14.

Kamakura, W., B. Kim and J. Lee (1996). "Modeling Preference and Structural Heterogeneity in Consumer Choice." *Marketing Science* 15 (2), 152-172.

Kolko, J. and M. E. Gazala (2005). *Demystifying Segmentation*. Boston: Forrester Research.

Kumar, V., R. Venkatesan and W. Reinartz (2006). "Knowing What to Sell, When and to Whom." *Harvard Business Review* 83 (March) 131-137.

Lal, R. and P. M. Carrolo (2002). "Harrah's Entertainment Inc." Harvard Business School Publishing Case # 9-502-011, 1-27.

Libai, B., D. Narayandas and C. Humby (2002). "Toward an Individual Customer Profitability Model." *Journal of Service Research* 5(1): 69-76.

Mittal, V. and W. Kamakura. "Satisfaction, Repurchase Intent, and Repurchase Behavior: Investigating the Moderating Effect of Customer Characteristics." *Journal of Marketing Research* 38 (February) 131-142.

Niraj, R., M. Gupta and C. Narasimhan (2001). "Customer Profitability in a Supply Chain." *Journal of Marketing* 65(3): 1-16.

Reinartz, W., J. Thomas and V. Kumar (2005). "Balancing Acquisition and Retention Resources to Maximize Customer Profitability." *Journal of Marketing* 69 (January), 63-79.

Rust, R., K. Lemon and V. Zeithaml (2004). "Return on Marketing: Using Customer Equity to Focus Marketing Strategy." *Journal of Marketing* 68(1): 109-127.

Rust, R. and P. Verhoef (2005). "Optimizing the Marketing Interventions Mix in Intermediate-Term CRM." *Marketing Science* 24(3): 477-489.

Rust, Roland T., Valarie A. Zeithaml and Katherine N. Lemon (2000). *Driving Customer Equity: How Customer Lifetime Value Is Reshaping Corporate Strategy.* New York: The Free Press.

Steenkamp, J.-B. and F. Ter Hofstede (2002). "International Market Segmentation: Issues and Perspectives." *International Journal of Research in Marketing* 19: 185-213.

Thomas, J. and U. Sullivan (2005). "Managing Marketing Communications with Multichannel Customers." *Journal of Marketing* 69(4): 239-251.

Venkatesan, R. and V. Kumar (2004). "A Customer Lifetime Value Framework for Customer Selection and Resource Allocation Strategy." *Journal of Marketing* 68(October): 106-125.

Wedel, M. and W. Kamakura (1998). *Market Segmentation Conceptual and Methodological Foundations.* Norwell, MA. Kluwer Academic Publishers.

Zeithaml, V., R. Bolton, J. Deighton, T. Keiningham, K. Lemon, and J. A. Peterson (2006). "Forward-Looking Focus: Can Firms Have Adaptive Foresight?" *Journal of Service Research.* Forthcoming.

Zeithaml, V., R. Rust and K. Lemon (2001). "The Customer Pyramid: Creating and Serving Profitable Customers." *California Management Review* 43 (Summer), 118-142.

doi:10.1300/J366v05n02_04

Customer Divestment

Vikas Mittal

University of Pittsburgh

Matthew Sarkees

University of Pittsburgh

SUMMARY. Customer lifetime value (CLV) models are designed to identify high-value customers to be retained. By implication, the remaining customers must be divested. This aspect of CLV management, customer divestment, has not been addressed in research. In this paper we describe the process of customer divestment, report a framework enabling firms to implement customer divestment (Mittal, Sarkees, and Murshed, 2006), and identify key issues associated with the customer divestment process. In doing so, we formulate some key research questions and an agenda for future research. doi:10.1300/J366v05n02_05 *[Article copies available for a fee from The Haworth Document Delivery Service: 1-800-HAWORTH. E-mail address: <docdelivery@haworthpress.com> Website: <http://www.HaworthPress.com> © 2006 by The Haworth Press, Inc. All rights reserved.]*

Vikas Mittal, PhD, is Professor, Joseph M. Katz School of Business, University of Pittsburgh, 360 Mervis Hall, Pittsburgh, PA 15260 (E-mail: vmittal@katz.pitt.edu).

Matthew Sarkees is a PhD candidate, Joseph M. Katz School of Business, University of Pittsburgh, 351 Mervis Hall, Pittsburgh, PA 15260 (E-mail: msarkees@katz.pitt.edu).

[Haworth co-indexing entry note]: "Customer Divestment." Mittal, Vikas, and Matthew Sarkees. Co-published simultaneously in *Journal of Relationship Marketing* (Best Business Books, an imprint of The Haworth Press, Inc.) Vol. 5, No. 2/3, 2006, pp. 71-85; and: *Customer Lifetime Value: Reshaping the Way We Manage to Maximize Profits* (ed: David Bejou, Timothy L. Keiningham, and Lerzan Aksoy) Best Business Books, an imprint of The Haworth Press, Inc., 2006, pp. 71-85. Single or multiple copies of this article are available for a fee from The Haworth Document Delivery Service [1-800-HAWORTH, 9:00 a.m. - 5:00 p.m. (EST). E-mail address: docdelivery@haworthpress.com].

KEYWORDS. Customer divestment, customer lifetime value, customer relationship management

INTRODUCTION

Customer lifetime value (CLV) models allow firms to identify opportunities to enhance customer portfolio profitability through the acquisition, development and retention of customer relationships (e.g., Reinartz, Thomas, & Kumar, 2005; Johnson & Selnes, 2004). Research suggests that CLV is a powerful metric for allocating firm resources (Venkatesan & Kumar, 2004). However, application of the CLV concept in firms is in its early stages (e.g., Gupta, Lehmann, & Stuart, 2004).

One aspect of CLV that receives very limited discussion in research and in practice is customer divestment. By design, CLV models force a firm to focus on "undesirable" customers. For instance, CLV research notes that many of the customers in a firm's portfolio make little, none, or negative contributions to firm value (e.g., Rust, Lemon, & Zeithaml, 2004). What should firms do with these customers? If firms must divest them, how should the divestment process be structured? Customer divestment is not costless. Moreover, without the inclusion of customer divestment costs, CLV estimates may be grossly inaccurate.

Yet, a discussion of proactive management of customer divestment or even inclusion of divestment costs in CLV models is absent in management thinking and practice. Customer divestment is an issue that cuts across functions and the fallout is not strictly confined to the marketing function. Academic research, which should provide leadership on customer divestment issues, its associated costs, and the process of managing divestment, is virtually non-existent. Morgan and Hunt (1994) include certain economic costs of divestment in their study of commitment and trust in relationships but indicate that more work is needed in this area. Lehmann (1999) points out that research is needed to better understand the relationship of divestment process and its effects on both the firm and its customers.

In this article we hope to address this gap by highlighting key issues associated with the customer divestment process. What is customer divestment? How does it affect CLV and the value of the firm? What are the strategic factors that influence the firm's ability to effectively manage the customer divestment process? Key research questions are noted throughout the discussion and an agenda for future research is discussed.

WHAT IS CUSTOMER DIVESTMENT?

Customer divestment is defined as the firm-initiated termination of service to an existing customer (Mittal, Sarkees, & Murshed, 2006). It is fundamentally different from concepts such as customer switching (e.g., Keaveney, 1995) or customer defection (e.g., Jones, Mothersbaugh, & Beatty, 2000) that are customer-initiated relationship terminations. Customer divestment should ideally be based on a comprehensive process that is systematic and reflective rather than an indiscriminate termination of relationship with so-called unprofitable customers (Mittal et al.). Unfortunately, firms typically fail to understand how to divest customers. This typically engenders negative outcomes such as unfavorable publicity (Sutter, 2003), customer retaliation (Gallagher & Kennedy, 1997), and negative word of mouth (Gitomer, 2003).

Why Divest Customers?

Firm-initiated customer divestment is a growing reality in both business-to-consumer and business-to-business environments (Mittal et al., 2006). Health care, insurance, financial services, professional services and retail are just a few of the industries where customer divestment is becoming more prevalent. Profitability is certainly a consideration in identifying customer divestment targets. For example, in recent years Dorothy Lane Markets, a midwestern grocery store chain, embarked on a campaign to actively eliminate all but its most loyal customers after noting that occasional customers actually lost money (Kirsner, 1999). The stores even stopped advertising in local newspapers. In the financial services industry Bank One CEO Jamie Dimon divested 33% of its loan portfolio due to a lack of customer profitability, redirected his resources and saved an estimated $1 billion (Tully, 2002).

Other factors such as a change in business strategy, government regulations, capacity constraints, employee morale and productivity can also motivate a firm to divest customers. For example, executives we interviewed in some of the large accounting firms explained to us that increased government reporting requirements from Enron-like accounting scandals in public companies coupled with a period of declining interest in accounting at the undergraduate university level, forced them to jettison clients because of lack of staff. In other cases, the decision to divest customers may be a response to regulatory issues, e.g., anti-trust regulation. Finally, troublesome and over-demanding customers that burden the firm's resources may be divestment targets, particularly in business-to-business service relationships. An executive from a large service firm told us, "It was a question of whether or not we wanted to keep our employees. The client was working them too hard and mutiny was upon us. We value our people more than profit so we gently told the client that we could no longer assist them."

Customer Divestment: A Continuum

Mittal et al. (2006) propose that when firms want to divest customers, they move along a continuum of actions: reassess, renegotiate, educate, migrate, resuscitate, and finally end the customer relationship. In this section, we briefly describe that continuum.

The customer divestment continuum enables a systematic exploration of the relationship with the customer identified as a divestment target to perhaps arrive at a more compatible exchange of value. The first step should be to thoroughly review the exchange relationship and find ways that can make it mutually beneficial to both the customer and the firm. In doing this, financial metrics such as current and future spending patterns should be supplemented by a broader, non-financial assessment of the company-customer relationship. Second, renegotiating the relationship parameters may help avoid divestment. Third, the customer can be migrated within the firm to products or services that provide a better fit for the customer's needs and a better value to the firm. These customers may also be transitioned to strategic partners that can better serve them.

If the previous three strategies are unable to resolve the value-incompatibility between the two parties, the firm can embark on a campaign to educate the customer about the underlying relationship structure. Educational efforts may be designed to: (1) manage customer expectations about the costs of the service; (2) increase customer understanding of how the service is provided; (3) increase customer participation; and (4) increase customer self-selection. The fifth phase, resuscitation, attempts to salvage the relationship by bundling or unbundling products or service. Perhaps the customer will accept an offering that is more compatible with the firm's resources. If a value incompatible relationship still exists after systematically working through these five phases, the firm may have no other choice but to divest the customer. Once this decision is made, the key is to help the customer to recognize that the decision (1) was reached with careful thought and discussion; (2) was made after taking several steps to reinforce, rebuild or create a more mutually beneficial exchange; and (3) is mutually beneficial as the firm is no longer able to meet the customer's needs without harming itself.

CUSTOMER DIVESTMENT AND CLV

Even after the customers are divested, the true CLV of the remaining base may only be revealed after allowing for a period of time for the firm to redirect its resources. Given this effort, both efficiency and revenue gains should accrue to the firm (Rust, Moorman, & Dickson, 2002). By focusing on higher value customers the firm should be able to enhance its revenue base. Moreover, because these higher value customers are a good fit with the firm's value proposition, the firm should be able to service them with a high degree of efficiency. Interactively, both revenue and efficiency gains should positively contribute to the long-term value of the firm (Mittal, Anderson, Sayrak, & Tadikamalla, 2005). In other words, though it may reduce the value of the customer portfolio in the short run, customer divestment can have positive long-term consequences for a firm's CLV. As such, the customer divestment concept will become increasingly important as managers and researchers consider ways to properly value the customer base. In this section, we look at several factors that have influenced the rise of customer divestment.

Integration of Customers and Firms

Today, customers are often seen as "co-producers" (Vargo & Lusch, 2004) and many argue that co-production with the customer is essential to enhancing firm value (Prahalad & Ramaswamy, 2000). Many customers want to be a part of the value creation process, both in business-to-business and in business-to-consumer environments. Consider that consumers under the age of 30 in the United States virtually grew up using the Internet. This generation uses chat rooms and online blogs to comment on products and services targeted to their customer segment. Alternatively, the baby boomer generation begins to retire in large numbers in the coming years. Medical concerns, government regulations, intergenerational issues and maintaining self-sufficiency are all important drivers of this segment's customer behavior that encourage them to provide feedback on products and services. Similarly, business-to-business customers want to participate in value creation because it helps both parties operate in a more efficient manner. This increased interaction facilitates an influx of information that allows firms to better segment their customers, recognizing not only potential high impact customers but also potential divestment targets based on their financial, social, and emotional commitment to the relationship.

Increased Focus on Long-Term Relationships

Academic researchers and marketing professionals recognize that long-term customer relationships can provide benefits. Customer commitment, loyalty, lower servicing costs, and higher customer switching costs are all believed to be outcomes of long-term relationships (e.g., Garbarino & Johnson, 1999; Morgan & Hunt, 1994). Therefore, allocating the right mix of resources to cultivate long-term relationships is essential to competitive success. An inefficient use of the firm's resources can focus attention on customers that add little or no value to the firm. Worse yet, firms can spend resources on customers that actually destroy value, mistakenly believing that there is potential for some future benefit. The focus on long-term relationships places an emphasis not only on those customers in a firm's portfolio who are contributing to firm value but also those who are not. Recognizing the increasingly competitive environment to lock-in beneficial long-term customer relationships, firms must find ways to enhance overall CLV by deleting non-value added or value destroying customers from their portfolios.

Advances in Information Technology and Analytical Techniques

Ongoing advancements in information technology are creating new methods for information gathering and analysis. Complex CLV models, customer relationship management software, database management and other breakthroughs in information technology have increased the firm's ability to segment its customer base. It is now easier for managers to see which customers are unprofitable (although *why* they are unprofitable is still not fully understood). Technology facilitates decisions about which customers to keep and which ones to divest.

The Increasing Influence of Marketing

Traditionally, marketing was viewed as a support function with its expenditures seen as a line item expense. Managers had a difficult time linking marketing investments to the firm's financial success. Today, marketing scholars are leading the effort to build theoretical and empirical links between marketing actions and a firm's bottom line. For instance, the financial impact of improving customer satisfaction is now well established (e.g., Mittal et al., 2005; Anderson, Rust, & Lehmann, 1994). Marketing models, particularly CLV models, can increasingly provide "hard" metrics to enable top management to make actionable strategic decisions. Efforts in this regard should elevate the status of marketing (e.g., Raju, 2005; Moorman & Rust, 1999). We believe that this trend will accelerate so that–similar to periodic reviews of financial portfolios–firms will systematically review their customer portfolio making customer divestment a strategic priority with real bottom-line impact.

FACTORS MODERATING THE FALLOUT FROM CUSTOMER DIVESTMENT

Customer divestment can trigger many negative emotions, feelings, and attitudes among those divested as well as other stakeholders (Mittal et al., 2006). The extent and severity of these negative consequences are contingent on several factors. Understanding these factors enables firms to better manage the divestment process and curtail potential negative fallout. In fact, effective management of the divestment process can position the firm for strong benefits such as migrating customers to other products and services that better match the firm's resource capabilities. In this section, we present factors that can potentially moderate the impact of customer divestment on customers.

Alternative Relationship

Some customers have a monogamous relationship with the firm but others have many relationships (Rust et al., 2004). It is likely that the emotional impact of customer divestment will be stronger for monogamous customers. For these customers, activities aimed at education and renegotiation may benefit them as well as the firm. If these activities precede the final divestment, the firm can benefit as the customer is now more aware of the firm's point of view. It may be that the customer and firm can be mutually satisfied by simply adjusting the level of service and price to be more compatible. For example, Federal Express discovered that its relationships with some of its larger customers were actually losing money. With many of them, Federal Express renegotiated a mutually beneficial relationship. Other customers who could not or would not renegotiate were asked by Federal Express to choose a new shipping carrier (Brooks 1999).

For customers who simultaneously maintain many relationships, the opportunity to migrate them to another product or service offering within the firm may have benefits. The incompatibility of the current relationship may simply be due to offerings that are not valued by the customer. If the firm cannot provide value-added benefits, a migration of these customers to an alternative, more beneficial relationship outside of the firm should be seriously considered. Though the firm may incur "transition costs" to migrate the customer to another relationship, it may–in the long run–be lower compared to the continued cost of carrying a non-valued added customer. Many firms transition customers to strategic partners. Hewlett-Packard announced the discontinuation of the production and service of certain products in mid-2002 (Hewlett-Packard press release, July 15, 2002). To ease customers' minds, Hewlett-Packard initiated a detailed migration strategy to its designated partner, BEA Systems, Inc. The plan called for assistance with the migration to BEA Systems, Inc. products and services as well as negotiated discounts with the new provider. The intent was to make the new relationship with BEA Systems, Inc. so appealing that customers would value not only the new opportunity but also Hewlett-Packard's effort in assisting them. Interesting questions surround the migration issue as it pertains to customer divestment such as: How much cost in the transition to a new provider should be borne by the divesting firm? What strategic partner agreements should the firm establish so that transition options are available for customers?

Divestment Warning

Firms that display extra effort are often rewarded by customers (Morales, 2005). We extend this concept to how firms manage the divestment process. As previously mentioned, before divestment occurs efforts should be undertaken to educate, renegotiate, and migrate the customer. Even after all of these steps, if the firm must divest a customer, the divestment–for the customer–should neither be sudden nor unexpected.

A warning notification that the relationship with the customer might be ended in the future not only represents a good faith effort, but also enables the customer to make alternative arrangements. Sarkees and Mittal (2006) examined customer reactions to divestment and found that warnings can mitigate the negative customer attitude and intent toward the firm.

Theoretically, a warning notification also shifts some of the control over the potential divestment to the customer: The customer becomes partially to blame if a termination event occurs. When customers recognize that they are at least partially to blame, they may be less inclined to find fault with a firm's actions (Folkes, 1984). This mitigates the negative impact on the firm's resources and brand image. Yet to be answered by research are issues such as the following: What type of warning should firms provide? Does warning type vary by customer segment? How many warnings should be given before actually ending the relationship?

The absence of pre-divestment warnings can hurt in several ways. First, the customer has no real opportunity to interact with the company to address the perceived issues. Angry customers can take up more time from employees through customer service calls and other interactions. Second, the divested customer has no transition time to find and to migrate to a new relationship. Third, blindsiding a customer with a divestment action increases the chances of retaliatory actions by the customer. The customer may feel a sense of embarrassment or a loss of self-esteem from the divestment. The firm may incur negative short- or long-term brand image impairment, depending upon the facts and circumstances surrounding the divestment.

Customer Resource Constraints

After hurricane Katrina, Nationwide and All-State announced that they would collectively divest approximately 130,000 customers whose properties are located in risky areas for hurricane damage (Sedore, 2005). This announcement was greeted by much negative press in the newspapers and comments from government regulators. If many insurance companies simultaneously engage in divestment initiatives, it is unlikely that a reasonable insurance plan can be found by many customers. More conceptual and empirical research is needed to understand customer divestment issues following natural "discontinuities" like these events. For instance, a spike in health-care expenditures after an accident, a death in the family or a sick family member may cause customers to default on credit card payments. Beyond offering temporary reprieve, how should credit card companies (or other creditors) understand and assist these customers? More importantly, how can customers and firms jointly plan for these events so that the possibility of divestment, especially sudden and involuntary from customers' perspective, can be minimized. Game theoretic models can be especially useful in developing insights into this issue. Other questions that need to be addressed include: What processes should the firm establish to handle the relationship under these circumstances? Besides fairness and empathy, what needs–financial, emotional, and social–would customers, front-line employees and firms have? What safety mechanisms–market-based and regulatory–are in place so that firms do not take advantage of such customers?

Besides acts of nature, there may be other circumstances that preclude customers from having a high CLV relationship with firms. Consider, for instance, categories that society views as universal service obligations. These services are basic necessities, even rights for citizens, and may include health care, access to safe housing, telephone services, and education. In other situations, particularly business-to-business settings, previous contractual agreements with other firms prevent customers from creating a mutually beneficial relationship.

Several complex questions are evident concerning divestment given customer resource constraints that the firm must answer. First, are customer resource constraints that prevent significant additional investment in the relationship with the firm temporary or permanent? What factors should the firm use to determine if the resource constraints are permanent or temporary and how must these assessments be factored in the divestment decision? What implications–financial, legal, social, and ethical–follow from the divestment decision? What, if anything, can the firm do to help alleviate the customer's constraints given that the firm wants to keep the relationship? Finally, how do firms collaborate with other members of the society–government, non-governmental organizations, and various other publics–to address the consumption needs of such customers? Naturally, if divestment must be carried out, the firm benefits by conducting itself accordingly and clearly explaining the circumstances to the divested customer and other interested/affected publics.

Technology Facilitates Divestment

Technology can affect and moderate the effect of customer divestment activities. For example, analysis of customer databases can help firms to better assess the customer base and pinpoint divestment targets. More importantly, technological advances pertaining to marketing channels can create new opportunities for firms to interact with customers, potentially eliminating the need for divestment. Technologies such ATMs and e-ticketing can reduce the cost of servicing customers thereby eliminating the need to divest them for profit-based reasons. Internet channels present an opportunity for firms to migrate customers targeted for divestment to channels in which services can be provided at a lower cost to the firm. Such migration can better match the company's resources with the customer's desired service level. For instance, Fidelity identified 25,000 customers who overused its call centers. By migrating them to the Internet for customer service needs, Fidelity was able to reduce the cost of service to them and thus retain most of these customers rather than having to divest them (Brady, 2000).

CUSTOMER DIVESTMENT AND CLV: KEY ISSUES

Divesting customers is a viable strategic option to improve firm value rather than a taboo management topic. Our in-depth interviews with managers indicate that in contractual business-to-business settings, divesting bad relationships is seen as a method to enhance firm value. Yet, in business-to-consumer environments, the customer appears to be largely in control of the relationship. Especially in business-to-consumer settings, it is critical for managers to fully understand the ramifications of embracing the customer divestment concept.

Equally important for managers is the establishment of sound policies that enable the implementation of the customer divestment concept within firms. Customer divestment is no different from other organizational initiatives that must be incorporated into practice. To be successful, top management must overcome organizational inertia, particularly mental inertia (Zeitz, Mittal, & McCauly, 1999). For instance, marketing managers are conditioned to think that a firm's overarching goal should be to acquire and to retain customers. Little or no thought is given to divesting customers. Yet, integrating this new idea into the core philosophies of the firm is essential for long-term success. To do this, firms should address issues related to people/employees as well as to divestment processes.

When financial services leader Marsh & McLennan recently divested thousands of clients, it gave virtually no warning to its employees (McDonald, 2005). Employee morale suffered and turnover increased. To mitigate such occurrences, firms should first create and facilitate a knowledge-sharing environment across functions so that customer divestment decisions are not a surprise to employees. There is also a need to train employees appropriately in the customer divestment processes so that mistakes that cause a negative impact on the firm do not occur. Similarly, firms should develop reward systems for employees who effectively manage "out" bad customer relationships. Firms should also be mindful to treat customers respectfully in the customer divestment process so that employees who work with a particular segment (e.g., low socioeconomic group) do not feel their customers are mistreated. In many situations, these employees have built relationships with those customers and have underlying personal feelings about the fairness or lack thereof of their firm's initiating divestment actions. We also believe that counsel should be provided to employees who have endured difficult customer divestment decisions.

Creating the right process infrastructure to support customer divestment is likely to be a more difficult challenge given that these initiatives cut across business functions. Overcoming process challenges, however, are nothing new to firms. For example, despite a decade of research supporting the benefits of increasing customer satisfaction, recent evidence notes that firms still vary widely in their customer satisfaction infrastructure (Morgan, Anderson, & Mittal, 2005). To become a key strategic option and priority for firms, processes that enhance inter- and intra-functional cooperation and coordination to identify divestment targets will be needed. More importantly, firms should establish clear guidelines for the customer divestment process. These guidelines should not be narrowly focused on profitability. Rather, they should address ethical, legal, and social aspects of engaging in the divestment continuum. An "appeals process" for both employees and customers should be part of customer divestment. Firms should create an ombudsman role within the firm to serve as an advocate for employees and customers. Despite the best efforts of employees during the divestment process, there will invariably be customers who want a "final hearing." Giving customers a last opportunity to correct the perceived inequity should prove beneficial for the firm.

Finally, firms must educate customers about the concept of customer divestment. For customer divestment to work efficiently and effectively, it is important to let customers know the firm's side of the exchange relationship. This will be difficult as customers do not normally expect that a firm will initiate the end to a relationship. Yet, expectations management is important to firm success (e.g., Oliver, 1980).

AGENDA FOR FUTURE RESEARCH

This article has presented a broad discussion of the customer divestment concept as well as some of the key research issues. These unanswered research questions should help frame future discussions of customer divestment, its effects on firms and customers, and public policy. Though they are not exhaustive, key customer divestment research issues are:

- What customer divestment factors, beyond profitability alone, should be included in a CLV calculation so that these inevitable costs to the firm are considered? Specifically, how to expand the CLV concept to include the social, emotional, and other non-financial benefits of customer-firms relationships?
- Related to the above, how (and how often) should these factors be measured, particularly the non-financial indicators?
- How do managers change traditional thinking that every customer should be retained? Similarly, how can researchers embrace the concept of customer divestment?
- What metrics should be created and monitored to better integrate the customer divestment ladder with CLV measurement? How do these relate to metrics of shareholder value (Tobin's q) in terms of efficiency and productivity and profitability?
- Research is needed to clearly identify and articulate the social, ethical, and legal impact of customer divestment decisions. Both long-term and short-term impacts on constituents like retained customers, employees, competitors, and the general public should be examined.
- What role do expectations, attributions, commitment, regret, and trust play in determining consumer reactions (e.g., perceptions of fairness) to divestment? How are current customers affected by the plight of those customers who are divested?
- What are the long-term effects on customers and firms of a widespread move toward divestment across industries? How do and how should competitors react to a divested customer? In what ways does divestment by one firm represent an opportunity for competitors?
- How do divestment decisions affect other financial aspects of the firm? For instance, what impact on fixed and variable costs, the ability to conduct customer-based experiments, and getting customer feedback do acts of customer divestment have?

- How can customer divestment be examined in the context of mergers and acquisitions?

These are some of the issues that should be examined by researchers. In this paper we have outlined the concept of customer divestment as it affects CLV. This idea is still in its infancy, something that is considered a taboo among marketing researchers and managers. We hope that this paper will stimulate further discussion of this concept, enabling us to better understand it in its entirety, and therefore enable thoughtful implementation of the same.

REFERENCES

Anderson, E.W., Fornell, C., & Lehmann, D.R. (1994). Customer satisfaction, market share, and profitability: findings from Sweden. *Journal of Marketing, 58,* 53-66.

Brady, D. (2000, October 23). Why service stinks. *Business Week, 3704,* 118-126.

Brooks, R. (1999, January 7). Alienating customers isn't always a bad idea, many firms discover. *Wall Street Journal–Eastern Edition, 233,* A1.

Folkes, V.S. (1984). Customer reactions to product failure: an attributional approach. *Journal of Consumer Research, 10,* 398-409.

Gallagher, S., & Kennedy, N. (1997, July). Is your bank trying to dump you? *Kiplinger's Personal Finance Magazine, 51,* 82-83.

Garbarino, E., & Johnson, M.S. (1999). The different roles of satisfaction, trust, and commitment in customer relationships. *Journal of Marketing, 63,* 70-87.

Gitomer, J. (2003, July 18). Why bad policies may result in 'firing' good customers. *Denver Business Journal.*

Gupta, S., Lehmann, D.R., & Stuart, J. (2004). Valuing customers. *Journal of Marketing Research, 41,* 7-18.

Johnson, M.D., & Selnes, F. (2004). Customer portfolio management: toward a dynamic theory of exchange relationships. *Journal of Marketing, 68,* 1-17.

Jones, M.A., Mothersbaugh, D.L., & Beatty, S.E. (2000). Switching barriers and repurchase intentions. *Journal of Retailing, 76,* 259-274.

Keaveney, S.M. (1995). Customer switching behavior in service industries: an exploratory study. *Journal of Marketing, 59,* 71-82.

Kirsner, S. (1999, June). Dorothy Lane loves its customers. *Fast Company, 25,* 76-77.

Lehmann, D.R. (1999). Consumer behavior and Y2K. *Journal of Marketing, 63,* 14-18.

McDonald, I. (2005, August 29). After Spitzer probe, Marsh CEO tries corporate triage. *Wall Street Journal–Eastern Edition, 246,* A1-A5.

Mittal, V., Sarkees, M.E., Murshed F. (2006). Do you know how to fire a customer? The customer divestment process. *Unpublished manuscript.*

Mittal, V., Anderson, E.W., Sayrak, A., & Tadikamalla, P. (2005). Dual emphasis and the long-term financial impact of customer satisfaction. *Marketing Science, 24,* 544-555.

Moorman, C.T., & Rust, R.T. (1999). The role of marketing. *Journal of Marketing, 63*, 180-197.

Morales, A.C. (2005). Giving firms an "e" for effort: consumer responses to high-effort firms. *Journal of Consumer Research, 31*, 806-812.

Morgan, N.A., Anderson, E.W., & Mittal, V. (2005), Understanding firms' customers satisfaction information usage. *Journal of Marketing, 69*, 131-151.

Morgan, R.M., & Hunt, S.D. (1994). The commitment-trust theory of relationship marketing. *Journal of Marketing, 58*, 20-38.

Oliver, R.L. (1980). A cognitive model of the antecedents and consequences of satisfaction decisions. *Journal of Marketing Research, 17*, 460-469.

Prahalad, C.K., & Ramaswamy, V. (2000). Co-opting customer competence. *Harvard Business Review, 78*, 79-87.

Raju, J.S. (2005). Revitalizing the role of marketing in business organizations: what can poor academics do to help? *Journal of Marketing, 69*, 17-19.

Reinartz, W.J., Thomas, J.S., & Kumar, V. (2005). Balancing acquisition and retention resources to maximize customer profitability. *Journal of Marketing, 69*, 63-79.

Rust, R.T., Lemon, K.N., & Zeithaml, V.A. (2004). Return on marketing: using customer equity to focus marketing strategy. *Journal of Marketing, 68*, 109-127.

Rust, R.T., Moorman, C.T., & Dickson, P.R. (2002). Getting return on quality: revenue expansion, cost reduction, or both? *Journal of Marketing, 66*, 7-24.

Sarkees, M.E., & Mittal, V. (2006). Mitigating negative customer reactions to relationship termination. *Unpublished manuscript*, University of Pittsburgh, Pittsburgh, PA.

Sedore, D. (2005, September 1). Nationwide dropping 35,000 policies. *The Palm Beach Post*.

Sutter, S. (2003, July 28). When a customer is wrong. *Marketing Magazine, 108*, 22-25.

Tully, S. (2002, July 22). The Jamie Dimon show. *Fortune, 146*, 88-96.

Vargo, S.L., & Lusch, R.F. (2004). Evolving to a new dominant logic for marketing. *Journal of Marketing, 68*, 1-17.

Venkatesan, R., & Kumar, V. (2004). A customer lifetime value framework for customer selection and resource allocation strategy. *Journal of Marketing, 68*, 106-125.

Zeitz, G., Mittal, V., & McCauly, B. (1999). Distinguishing adoption and entrenchment of management practices: a framework for analysis. *Organization Studies, 20*, 741-776.

doi:10.1300/J366v05n02_05

Customer Lifetime Value
and Firm Valuation

Sunil Gupta

Columbia University

Donald R. Lehmann

Columbia University

SUMMARY. Unlike most marketing metrics, CLV provides information which is directly relevant to marketing decision makers, non-marketing executives such as CFOs, and financial analysts. This paper highlights why and how CLV is financially relevant. It explicitly compares CLV-based valuation with four finance-oriented methods (DCF, P/E ratio, customer counting, and extrapolation). We also discuss implications for marketing managers, financial executives as well as educators. doi:10.1300/J366v05n02_06 *[Article copies available for a fee from The Haworth Document Delivery Service: 1-800-HAWORTH. E-mail address: <docdelivery@haworthpress.com> Website: <http://www.HaworthPress.com> © 2006 by The Haworth Press, Inc. All rights reserved.]*

Sunil Gupta, PhD, is Meyer Feldberg Professor of Business, Columbia Business School, Columbia University, New York, NY 10027 (E-mail: sg37@columbia.edu).

Donald R. Lehmann, PhD, is George E. Warren Professor of Business, Columbia Business School, Columbia University, New York, NY 10027 (E-mail: drl2@columbia.edu).

[Haworth co-indexing entry note]: "Customer Lifetime Value and Firm Valuation." Gupta, Sunil, and Donald R. Lehmann. Co-published simultaneously in *Journal of Relationship Marketing* (Best Business Books, an imprint of The Haworth Press, Inc.) Vol. 5, No. 2/3, 2006, pp. 87-110; and: *Customer Lifetime Value: Reshaping the Way We Manage to Maximize Profits* (ed: David Bejou, Timothy L. Keiningham, and Lerzan Aksoy) Best Business Books, an imprint of The Haworth Press, Inc., 2006, pp. 87-110. Single or multiple copies of this article are available for a fee from The Haworth Document Delivery Service [1-800-HAWORTH, 9:00 a.m. - 5:00 p.m. (EST). E-mail address: docdelivery@haworthpress.com].

KEYWORDS. Customer lifetime value, intangible assets, valuation, market value, mathematical models

INTRODUCTION

Peter Drucker, the late management guru, said, "Innovation and marketing are the only two valuable activities of a firm. The rest are costs." Yet, marketing has come under increasing pressure as executives find it difficult to show a return on marketing spending. It is easy to ask for millions of dollars for advertising or for improving customer service, but much harder to show how this investment affects firm profits or shareholder value. This has often led firms to resort to proven short-term strategies such as promotions, cost-cutting or financial reengineering whose effects are easier to quantify.

Improving traditional marketing metrics such as brand awareness, attitudes or even sales and share does not guarantee a return on marketing investment. In fact, marketing actions that improve sales or share may actually harm the long-run sales and profitability of a brand. (e.g., Mela, Gupta and Lehmann 1997; Jedidi, Mela and Gupta 1999).

Recently, the concept of customer lifetime value (CLV) has gained increasing importance among both academics and practitioners. Companies such as Harrah's have had tremendous success managing their businesses based on CLV and database techniques. Academics have written scores of articles and books on this topic (Rust, Zeithaml and Lemon 2000; Blattberg, Getz and Thomas 2001; Gupta and Lehmann 2005). The growing interest in this concept is due to several reasons. First, CLV forces a company to be customer-centric. Second, by its very definition, it focuses on long-term profitability instead of share or sales. Third, it allows a firm to assess the value of individual customers and target them through customized offerings. Fourth, the improvement in information technology and the availability of customer-level transaction data permits companies to perform detailed analyses instead of relying on aggregate survey-based measures such as satisfaction.

Customer lifetime value depends on three main components–acquisition, retention, and cross-selling or margin expansion. Most of the focus in the CLV literature has been on building better models for these components. In terms of applications, the emphasis has been on customer selection (which customers to acquire), campaign management (which catalog to send to which customer), customer retention efforts (who is likely to defect and what can we do to prevent it), cross-selling efforts (what do we sell to whom at what time), and resource allocation (how much resources do we allocate to acquisition versus retention).

While this focus of CLV is helpful in making marketing more accountable and assessing its return on investment, it is still tactical from top management's perspective. In other words, neither Wall Street nor the CEO really wants to know which customers should get which catalogs. Does it mean that they should not care about CLV? In this paper we argue that they should. Specifically, we show that CLV can and has been linked to firm value. In many situations it complements the existing financial approaches to firm valuation, while in others CLV may be the only way to get a good estimate of a firm's worth.

The plan for the paper is as follows. We start with a discussion of various valuation approaches used in finance and by Wall Street. In this discussion we highlight the situations where traditional financial methods either fail or have a hard time getting a reasonable estimate of firm value. Next, we discuss how CLV bridges the gap between marketing and finance. This is followed by a discussion of how CLV can be used to value a firm. We start this discussion with an intuitive explanation and a case study. This is followed by a formal model and its results. Next, we highlight recent advances and limitations of this approach. We conclude with the implications of linking CLV and firm value for practitioners of marketing and finance as well as educators.

TRADITIONAL VALUATION APPROACHES

At the risk of oversimplifying, we briefly describe four approaches that are used in finance and by Wall Street.

Discounted Cash Flow (DCF) Approach

The gold standard for valuation is the discounted cash flow or DCF approach which posits that the value of a firm is the discounted sum of all future cash flows (Brealey and Myers 1996). Frequently this is implemented by estimating future cash flow up to a finite time period (e.g., eight years) and adding a "terminal value" of the firm to them. This approach works well for stable businesses where it is easy to forecast the future cash flows and the terminal value does not have a large impact on firm value. However, high-growth companies or firms in the early stages of their life cycle (e.g., Google, XM Radio) have limited history to draw on for future projections. Further, most of the value of these companies is based on future growth which makes estimates of terminal value critical. In some cases (e.g., XM Radio or Amazon in the late 1990s), the firms do not even have positive cash flow. Therefore it becomes extremely difficult, if not impossible, to use current negative cash flows to project positive cash flows in the future.

In spite of these challenges, the DCF approach has been used to value high growth companies. For example, Damodaran (2001) used this approach and estimated Amazon's share price value as $34.37 in June 2000. Damodaran's approach has five main inputs. First, revenue growth for the company is estimated. For Amazon, Damodaran estimated that the current annual revenue growth of 120% would drop to 5% by year 10, giving a compound annual growth of 40%. Second, you need to forecast operating margin. This is a challenging task given that the operating margin for Amazon at that time was −16.27%. Damodaran assumed that Amazon would reach an operating margin of 9.32%, the average for the specialty retailing industry, by the end of the tenth year. Third, he estimated (based on the industry average) that for every $3 in additional sales, Amazon would need to reinvest $1 in capital. Finally he estimates the beta for Amazon and its debt ratio. These assumptions helped him use the DCF approach to arrive at a $34.37 per share price for Amazon. While this estimate may be reasonable and intuitive, the assumptions needed to arrive at the valuation raise questions and need justification.

Price-Earnings Approach

Another approach, which has a strong link with the DCF approach, is the price-earnings or the P/E ratio. The price of a stock is based on the expectations of the future dividends as well as capital appreciation of the stock. Dividends are a fraction of the company earnings that are paid to the shareholders. Assuming a dividend payout ratio of 1 and a constant growth in earnings, it is easy to show that

$$\frac{P}{E} = \frac{1}{i-g} \qquad (1)$$

where P is the current stock price, E is the current earnings, P/E is the price-earnings ratio, i is the discount rate, and g is the growth rate of earnings. Assuming a discount rate of 10%, this suggests that for a company with no growth prospects, the P/E ratio is about 10. With 5% expected growth, P/E is 20, close to the recent average for S&P 500 stocks. This approach is highly dependent on a good estimate of growth rate (g). Further, it runs into problems for companies in the early stages of their life cycle–it is hard to estimate the P/E ratio for a firm that has no E.

The Internet-Era Approach

The inability of the DCF and P/E approaches to value Internet firms in the late 1990s led several Wall Street analysts to use other methods. The approach of estimating market size, firm share in that market, its profit margin and P/E ratio is well-accepted in the financial community. However, there is a high degree of subjectivity involved in estimating many factors such as market share, profit margin, etc. Henry Blodget became famous in late 1998 for predicting that Amazon's share price would reach $400. Blodget justified this valuation based on the following. He first estimated the total market for books, music and videos to be around $100 billion. He then estimated that, similar to Wal-Mart, Amazon would become a category leader and attain a 10% share, thus giving it revenue of $10 billion. Although traditional retailers generally achieve a net margin of 1% to 4%, Blodget also estimated that Amazon's leaner operation would fetch it a fatter margin of 7% or $700 million. Next, Blodget estimated a P/E ratio of anywhere between 10 (for a slow growth scenario) to 75 (for a fast growing scenario), thus giving Amazon as high a market cap as $53 billion or $332 per share (Fortune 1999).

In a variant of this approach, Desmet et al. (2000) created various scenarios for Amazon with market share from 5% to 15% and operating margin of 7% to 14%. They assigned subjective probabilities for these scenarios and arrived at an expected valuation for Amazon at $23 billion.

The Eye Ball Approach

The difficulty of valuing high growth companies, such as dot coms, by traditional methods led to a series of new metrics and methods. One of the popular measures to emerge was based on the number of customers or eyeballs. The popularity of this metric was based on the observation that growth companies need to acquire customers rapidly in order to gain first mover advantage and build network externalities, regardless of the cost involved (*Wall Street Journal*, Nov 22, 1999). Academic research also provided validation for this. For example, Trueman,

Wong and Zhang (2001) combined financial information from financial statements with the non-financial information from Media Metrix to predict the market value of 63 Internet firms from September 1998 to December 1999. While net income had no relationship with stock price, both unique visitors and page views added significant explanatory power. Demers and Lev (2001) used similar data for 84 Internet companies for 1999-2000. They found that non-financial measures such as reach (i.e., number of unique visitors) and stickiness (i.e., site's ability to hold its customers) explained share prices of Internet companies, both before and after the bursting of the bubble.

Note that these studies were correlational in nature and assumed that the market value represents the true intrinsic value of the firm at any time–an efficient market argument. However, even if the markets are efficient in the long run, recent history suggests significant deviations exist in the short run. In other words, the value of the dependent variable in these studies is likely to change significantly over time which obviously alters the value placed on the number of customers. As a reaction to the collapse of the Internet stock market bubble, financial analysts are now quite skeptical about non-financial metrics, especially number of customers. For example, a *Fortune* article criticized a Wall Street icon, Mary Meeker, for overly relying on eyeballs and page views versus traditional financial measures (*Fortune*, May 14, 2001).

MARKETING MEETS FINANCE

Given the skepticism about the usefulness of marketing metrics, how can marketing be relevant to finance, especially when it has difficulty documenting the return on investment for its own programs (e.g., advertising)? We believe that CLV can bridge this gap. CLV not only makes marketing more accountable but also provides a fundamental tool to help value firms.

The traditional focus of marketing has been to provide better value to the customer through better service, products, convenience, delivery and so on. Metrics used to gauge the success of marketing programs include awareness, attitude and customer satisfaction. Not surprising, hundreds of articles have been written about how to measure satisfaction and its antecedents. However, it is difficult to know how much a company should spend to move its customer satisfaction rating from, say, 4.2 to 4.3 on a 5-point scale.

The Two-Sides of Customer Value

Gupta and Lehmann (2005) argue that we need to examine two sides of customer value–the value a firm provides to its customers (the traditional marketing view) and the value customers provide to the firm (the finance view). In a way, these two sides capture the different philosophies of marketing (the customer is king) and finance (cash is king). A company allocating its resources needs to consider both sides of customer value. Customers who do not provide much value to the firm (low CLV) but get a large value from the firm may be considered free riders, i.e., they derive a large benefit without providing much in return. In some cases, a firm may be better off either raising prices for these customers or the resources devoted to them. Customers who are low on both types of value may, ceteris paribus, be worth shedding. In other words, more customers or a higher market share may not be necessarily good for a firm. Best Buy recognized this and cut back the resources denoted to its low value customers.

A firm can invest money in its customers by providing better value to them. The reason for doing this is to get a greater return from them so that they will provide current and future profits to the firm (as measured by their CLV). This perspective not only makes marketing more accountable (i.e., programs are evaluated in terms of their impact on CLV) but also suggests that marketing expenditures should be viewed as investments (just like R&D) rather than expenses.

Estimating CLV

CLV is the present value of all future profits obtained from a customer over his/her life of relationship with a firm. CLV is thus a form of the discounted cash flow approach used in finance with two key differences. First, CLV is typically defined and estimated at an individual customer or segment level. Second, CLV explicitly incorporates the possibility that a customer may defect to competitors in the future.

The CLV for a single customer is (Gupta, Lehmann and Stuart 2004; Reinartz and Kumar 2003),

$$CLV = \sum_{t=0}^{T} \frac{(p_t - c_t)r_t}{(1+i)^t} - AC \qquad (2)$$

where, p_t = price paid by a consumer at time t,

c_t = direct cost of servicing the customer at time t,

i = discount rate or cost of capital for the firm,

r_t = probability of customer repeat buying or being "alive" at time t,

AC = acquisition cost,

T = time horizon for estimating CLV.

Researchers have used a number of variations in modeling and estimating CLV. For example, some have used an arbitrary time horizon or *expected* customer lifetime (Reinartz and Kumar 2000; Thomas 2001), while others have used an infinite time horizon (e.g., Gupta, Lehmann and Stuart 2004; Fader, Hardie and Lee 2005). Gupta and Lehmann (2003, 2005) also show that if margins (p-c) and retention rates (r) are constant over time and we use an infinite time horizon, then CLV simplifies to the following expression:

$$CLV = \sum_{t=0}^{\infty} \frac{(p-c)r}{(1+i)^t} = m \frac{r^t}{(1+i-r)} \tag{3}$$

In other words, CLV is simply the margin (m) times a *margin multiple* (r/1 + i − r). When the retention rate is 90% and the discount rate is 12%, the margin multiple is about four. Gupta and Lehmann (2005) show how equation (3) can be modified when margin and retention rates are not constant.

As mentioned earlier, CLV is influenced by three main components–acquisition, retention and margin or cross-selling. Researchers either build separate models for these three components or combine two or more of these components. For example, Thomas (2001), and Reinartz, Thomas and Kumar (2005) simultaneously capture customer acquisition and retention. Fader, Hardie and Lee (2005) capture recency and frequency in one model and build a separate model for monetary value. Gupta et al. (2006) provide a detailed discussion of the various modeling approaches for modeling CLV.

LINKING CLV TO FIRM VALUE

How can the simple micro-level concept of CLV address firm-level issues such as the stock price or firm value? The premise, shown in Figure 1, is very simple. The value of a firm is based on its current and

FIGURE 1. Linking Customer Value and Firm Value

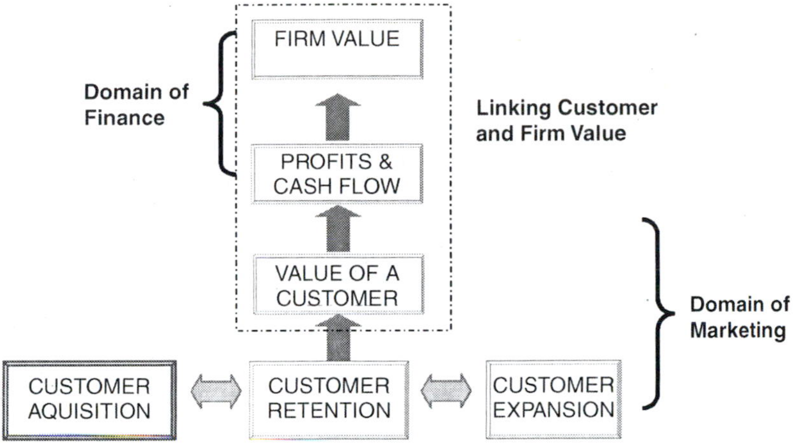

Used with permission. Gupta and Lehmann (2005), *Managing Customers as Investments*, Wharton Publishing, page 80.

future cash flow. Estimating future cash flow has traditionally been the domain of finance. Financial analysts generally are entrusted with projecting a firm's future cash flow, estimating a firm's cost structure and discount rate, and then arriving at the firm's market value and stock price, based on methods such as discounted cash flow (DCF) analysis.

In contrast, marketing has traditionally focused on meeting customer needs and designing programs to provide greater value to its customer than competitors. Customer lifetime value provides a critical link between marketing decisions and firm value. With the exception of pure financial activities, such as currency transactions, all the profits and cash flows (which form the basis of firm valuation) come from customers buying the products and services of a firm. If we can assess the lifetime value of one customer, then we can also estimate the value of the entire current customer base. For example, if the average CLV of a customer for a company is $100 and it has 30 million customers, then the value of its current customers is $3 billion. This value is sometimes called *static customer equity*. Clearly the value of a firm is highly dependent on its future growth. Knowledge of customer acquisition and retention rates enables us to estimate the number and value of future customers. In other words, the value of a single customer provides the building block for forecasting the cash flow–and hence the value–of a firm. As such, it should be the meeting ground and a common language between marketing and finance. Based on this simple premise, we show how CLV can be used for firm valuation.

From a financial analysts view, the key is to project the future growth of the company as was highlighted in the discussion of the P/E ratio. Methods of projecting growth often use linear extrapolations. For example, it is common for financial analysts to take the average growth rate of the last five years and assume that the growth rate will be the same in the future. While sometimes accurate, these assumptions do not rest on business fundamentals (i.e., acquisition, retention, and expansion rates and costs). In the case of new businesses this approach is even worse. For firms with negative earnings, how do you project future earnings or justify a P/E ratio when E is negative? Using CLV and projecting its components can alleviate this problem. In other words, CLV-based projections are based on business fundamentals which not only can help produce better forecasts but also provide better diagnostics (e.g., identify which factors affect firm value the most). We next illustrate this with a case study about valuation of Netflix.

Valuing Netflix

Netflix Inc. provides an online entertainment subscription service in the United States. Members have the choice of eight subscription plans, starting at $9.99 per month for unlimited rentals with one DVD out at a time. With the most popular plan of $17.99 a month, members rent as many DVDs as they want and keep them as long as they want, with three movies out at a time. There are no due dates, late fees, or shipping charges. Subscribers have access to a comprehensive library of more than 55,000 movies, television shows, and other filmed entertainment titles. Once a title has been returned, the company mails the next available title in a subscriber's request queue. The company, founded in 1998 with the idea of capitalizing on customer anger over late fees charged by Blockbuster and other competitors, grew at a rapid rate and by December 2003, had almost 1.5 million subscribers. The subscriber base increased to 2.6 million by the end of 2004 and to 4.2 million at the end of 2005. It is one of the few Internet-based companies that successfully went public after the bursting of the Internet bubble. Since its initial public offering in May 2002 when its stock price was under $10, its stock has performed well if a bit ironically. The stock price reached a high of $40 in January 2004, dipped to a low of $10 in early 2005 and as of February 2, 2006 trades at $27.

Netflix's primary business is subscriber-based. In 2005 its revenue was $688 million and its net income was $41.9 million. As of February 2, 2006 the company has a market value of $1.48 billion and a P/E ratio of 42.48. (Clearly the financial market is betting on the rapid growth of Netflix.[1])

Its financial statements reveal the following subscriber-based information. The average revenue per subscriber is about $18 per month (almost equal to the price of its most popular pricing plan). Its gross margin is 47.1% and other variable costs (e.g., fulfillment, etc.) are 13.9%, giving it a margin of about 33.2% or about $71.71 per year.[2] The churn rate of Netflix subscribers is 4.3% per month, which is equivalent to an annual retention rate of about $(1-0.043)^{12}$ or about 59%. Assuming a 12% discount rate, this gives a subscriber CLV of approximately $80. With 4.2 million customers, this is equivalent to $336 million pre-tax value or almost $208 million post-tax (assuming a 38% corporate tax rate). Given Netflix's current market value of about $1.48 billion, this implies that the bulk of its value ($1.272 billion) has to come from future customers.

Netflix's average customer acquisition cost is about $40. This implies that the CLV of its newly acquired customers will be $80 − $40 or $40. Using this CLV and a 12% discount rate, it is easy to show that if Netflix acquires 1 million additional customers well into the future, their value will be ($40*1 million)/0.12 or $333 million pre-tax, or ($333*0.68 or $227 million post-tax). Put differently, Netflix has to acquire almost 5.6 million customers every year for a long time to justify its current valuations.

Is this rate of growth achievable? This is a matter of judgment that analysts and experts can debate based on their knowledge of the industry. Netflix acquired 1.2 million customers in 2004 and 1.6 million customers in 2005. Consequently, it is a bit optimistic to expect it to continue to add 5.6 million customers annually for many years. Potential competition from other companies (e.g., Amazon) as well as new technologies (e.g., DVD on demand or downloadable movies from iTunes) make this even more difficult to envision. Regardless of what you believe, however, this method makes valuation systematic and allows us to question and debate the basic assumptions built into it.

In this discussion, we simply estimated the required growth in subscribers to justify current valuation. Alternatively, we can build a formal

model to forecast the future growth in subscribers and other components that go as input into CLV as we do in the next section.

Customer-Based Valuation Model

Here we briefly describe the model proposed by Gupta, Lehmann
and Stuart (2004). The basic elements of the model are as follows. The
CLV for an existing customer is given by equation (2). In addition to existing customers, it is necessary to estimate future customer acquisitions, i.e., customers who join in year 1, 2, 3, etc. If n_1 customers join in
year 1, n_2 in year 2 and so on, then, ignoring when it is acquired, the
value of cohort k in the year its customers join the company is simply
n_k * Average CLV_k. Since this is the value of customers' k-years in the
future, the present value can be obtained by discounting this to the current year, i.e. $(n_k * CLV_k)/(1 + i)^k$. This translates into the following
equation:

$$Value = \sum_{k=0}^{\infty} \frac{n_k}{(1+i)^k} \sum_{t=k}^{\infty} m_{t-k} \frac{r^{t-k}}{(1+i)^{t-k}} - \sum_{k=0}^{\infty} \frac{n_k c_k}{(1+i)^k} \qquad (4)$$

where, n_k = number of customer in cohort k,
 m_t = annual margin provided by a customer at time t
 i = discount rate or cost of capital for the firm,
 r = probability of customer repeat buying or being "alive,"
 c_k = acquisition cost of cohort k.

Formula (4) assumes the retention rate is constant over time which is
equivalent to a constant hazard rate or the exponential "death" rate that
has been used by other researchers. For example, Schmittlein, Morrison
and Colombo (1987) and Fader, Hardie and Lee (2005) use a NBD/
Pareto model which assumes exponential death rate of consumers.
Gupta et al. also show that equation (4) can be recast into a continuous time frame, which is sometimes easy to estimate empirically:

$$Value = \int_{k=0}^{\infty} \int_{t=k}^{\infty} n_k m_{t-k} e^{-ik} e^{-\left(\frac{1+i-r}{r}\right)(t-k)} dt \, dk - \int_{k=0}^{\infty} n_k c_k e^{-ik} dk \qquad (5)$$

The next step is to model the components of equation (4) or (5).

Number of Customers

The growth in number of customers for Netflix (Figure 2) shows a typical diffusion pattern. Gupta et al. found a similar pattern in their study of five companies. They suggested that the cumulative number of customers N_t at any time t could be modeled as

$$N_t = \frac{\alpha}{1+ \exp(-\beta-\gamma t)} \qquad (6)$$

This S-shaped function asymptotes to α as time goes to infinity. The parameter γ captures the slope of the curve. The number of new customers acquired at any time is,

$$n_t = \frac{dN_t}{dt} = \frac{\alpha\gamma \exp(-\beta-\gamma t)}{[1+ \exp(-\beta-\gamma t)]^2} \qquad (7)$$

This model, also called the Technological Substitution Model, has been used by several researchers in modeling innovations and to project the

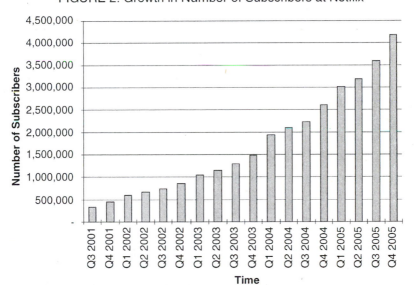

FIGURE 2. Growth in Number of Subscribers at Netflix

Source: Company records and financial statements

number of customers (e.g., Fisher and Pry 1971, Kim, Mahajan and Srivastava 1995). Alternatively, the well-known Bass (1969) model can be used to forecast future customers.

Margin

Several authors have assumed that margins for a customer remain constant over time. Reinartz and Kumar (2003) used average contribution margin of a customer based on his/her prior purchase behavior to project CLV. Gupta, Lehmann and Stuart (2004) also used a constant margin based on history which in many industries may be a reasonable assumption (Gupta and Lehmann 2005).

Venkatesan and Kumar (2004) used a simple regression model to capture changes in contribution margin over time. Specifically, they suggest that change in contribution margin for customer j at time t is

$$\Delta CM_{jt} = \beta X_{jt} + e_{jt} \tag{8}$$

Several studies also model cross-selling, which improves customer margin over time. For example, Verhoef, Franses and Hoekstra (2001) used an ordered probit model to describe consumers' cross-buying. Knott, Hayes and Neslin (2002) used logit, discriminant analysis and neural network models to predict the next product to buy and found that all models performed roughly the same and significantly better than random guessing. Knott et al. complemented their logit model which addresses what product a customer is likely to buy next, with a hazard model which addresses the question of when customers are likely to buy this product. They found that adding the hazard model improved projected profits by 25%.

Retention

Customer retention is the probability of a customer being "alive" or repeat buying from a firm. In contractual settings (e.g., cellular phones, magazine subscriptions), customers "inform" the firm when they terminate their relationship. However, in non-contractual settings (e.g., buying books from Amazon), a firm has to infer whether a customer is still active. Most companies define a customer as active based on simple rules-of-thumb. For example, eBay defines a customer as active if s/he has bid, bought or listed on its site during the last 12 months. While researchers who do not have access to individual level transaction data (e.g., Gupta et al. 2004) have used these industry estimates, others rely on customer transaction data and statistical models to assess the probability of retention.

Schmittlein, Morrison and Colombo (1987) assumed that a customer's transactions can be approximated by a Poisson distribution, his death rate by an exponential distribution, and consumer heterogeneity by gamma distributions. With these assumptions they arrived at a NBD/Pareto model. This model requires recency and frequency of consumer purchases to predict a consumer's probability of being alive in the certain time period and has been used by many researchers (e.g., Fader, Hardie and Lee 2005). This approach implicitly assumes a constant death rate (i.e., an exponential distribution) and ignores the impact of covariates or company actions. A related approach explicitly models consumer hazard rates as a function of covariates such as a proportional hazard model where the hazard rate (λ) is defined as a function of baseline hazard rate (λ_0) and covariates (X),

$$\lambda(t;X) = \lambda_0(t)\exp(\beta X) \qquad (9)$$

Different specifications for the baseline hazard rate provide different duration models such as exponential, Weibull or Gompertz. This approach was used by Bolton (1998), Gonul, Kim and Shi (2000), and Knott, Hayes and Neslin (2002).

Instead of modeling time duration, one can model customer retention or churn as a binary outcome (e.g., the probability of a wireless customer defecting in the next month). This is a form of discrete-time hazard model. Typically the model takes the form of a logit or probit. Due to its simplicity and ease of estimation, this approach is commonly used in the industry. Neslin et al. (2006) describe models of this type which were submitted by academics and practitioners as part of a "predicting churn tournament."

Some researchers have also modeled customer retention through Markov transition matrices. These models estimate transition probabilities of a customer being in a certain state. Bitran and Mondschein (1996) defined transition states based on RFM measures while Pfeifer and Carraway (2000) defined them based on customers' recency of purchases as well as an additional state for new or former customers.

CUSTOMER VALUE AND FIRM VALUE

How good are the estimates from the customer-based valuation approach? Gupta et al. (2004) used publicly available data from five companies to estimate the value of their current and future customers. The estimates were obtained by the method described earlier and compared with the market value of the companies (Figure 3). Libai, Muller and Peres (2006) replicated the analysis for these five companies using more recent data and found similar results. The results show that for three of the five companies, customer value provides a good proxy for firm value. The exceptions are Amazon and eBay. There are many potential reasons for the discrepancy, and we return to this issue later in our discussion of limitations and future research.

What drives firm value? Figure 4 shows the results obtained by Gupta et al. (2004). These results show that customer retention is the most important marketing lever. Specifically, a 1% improvement in customer retention improves customer value (which is a close proxy of firm value) by about 5%. In contrast, a similar improvement in margins boosts customer value by only about 1%. Improvements in acquisition costs have the smallest impact on value.

These results also highlight the relative importance of marketing and financial instruments. They suggest that a 1% improvement in retention rate has almost five times greater impact on firm value compared to a similar improvement in discount rate or cost of capital. In other words, firms will be better off redirecting their energy and resources from financial engineering to customer service and customer retention.

FIGURE 3. Customer Value and Firm Value (as of March 2002)

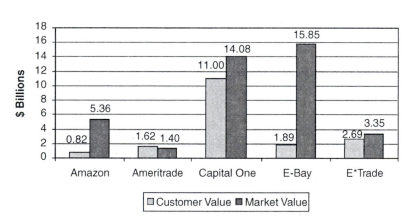

Used with permission. Gupta and Lehmann (2005), *Managing Customers as Investments*, Wharton Publishing, page 98.

FIGURE 4. Drivers of Customer and Firm Value

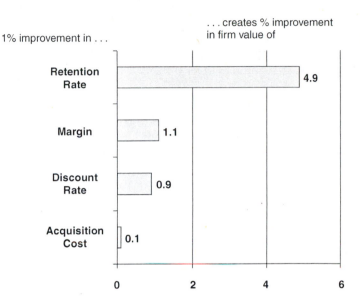

Used with permission. Gupta and Lehmann (2005), *Managing Customers as Investments*, Wharton Publishing, page 100.

IMPLICATIONS FOR MANAGERS

Customer metrics such as CLV and their link to firm value have significant implications for marketing managers, financial executives including financial analysts, and marketing educators.

Implications for Marketing Managers

Marketing managers have come under increasing pressure in many companies. Recent studies show that of all the senior managers in a company, the Chief Marketing Officer or CMO has the shortest tenure. This is partly due to their inability to show return on marketing investments. Marketing managers typically use metrics such as brand awareness, attitude, or satisfaction, which mean little to financial executives. Customer lifetime value bridges the gap between marketing and finance executives and between line and senior managers.

A focus on CLV suggests that marketing managers need to do three things. First, they need to measure customer-based metrics such as acquisition, retention and expansion. Sales and share are not the relevant measures–in the extreme one could get 100% share with no profits to show for it (something that happened to several firms during the dot com era). In other words, as shown in Table 1 below, the metrics for success need to change from sales and share to retention and CLV.

Second, marketing managers should focus on establishing the links between marketing actions and components of CLV. It is quite likely that some of the traditional measures influence these components. For example, satisfaction in general leads to greater retention. However, a focus on CLV suggests that it is not enough to monitor satisfaction and call it a success if these scores improve. It is imperative for a marketing manager to link the improvement in satisfaction scores to retention and CLV. Only then can s/he assess the return on investment.

Third, marketing managers need to use a language that bridges the gap between marketing and finance. It is easier to communicate the impact of marketing programs in terms of customer profitability and its impact on firm value than by discussing brand awareness or customer satisfaction scores.

Implications for Finance Executives and Financial Analysts

Finance executives are used to dealing with aggregate metrics such as profits, cash flows, earnings, etc. However, these aggregate measures do not provide the necessary diagnostics to understand the health of a business or how to grow it in the future. Two companies with the same current earnings and cash flow may have very different customer retention rates. For example, even though companies may look identical based on aggregate financial metrics, the firm with higher customer retention rate probably has a better future. Since research shows a strong link between customer and firm value, financial executives and analysts

TABLE 1

Traditional Metrics	Customer Metrics
Sales/Share	Customer acquisition (rate, cost)
Price, % sold on deal	Customer margin (dollar, growth)
Satisfaction	Customer retention (rate, cost)
Product profitability	Customer lifetime value

should actively monitor customer metrics such as acquisition and retention rates.

As intangible assets form a larger and larger part of a firm value, it is even more important that these assets be reflected on the balance sheet and other financial statements. This view was reinforced by SEC a few years ago:

> Intangible assets are hard to see and even harder to fix a precise value for. But a widening consensus is growing that the importance of (intangible) assets–from brand names and customer lists . . .–means that investors need to know more about them. A task force appointed by SEC will encourage companies to provide more information regarding those assets. *New York Times*, May 22, 2001

Customer metrics also serve an important role for financial analysts for whom the key is to project earnings growth. Past methods were generally linear extrapolations. How do you project future earnings or justify a P/E ratio when E is negative? One answer (implicitly applied at least to some extent by some analysts) is to project CLV and its components. If nothing else, a customer-based valuation method provides an alternative forecasting mechanism to the simple (and often linear) historical projection of cash flow.

It is encouraging to see that the markets are already moving in this direction. For example, companies such as Netflix, XM radio, and telecommunication companies routinely present customer metrics to financial analysts. Investment banks are also beginning to use customer-based valuation methods. For example, CSFB recently issued a report on its recommendation for Satellite radio companies (XM and Sirius). This analysis was largely based on estimating CLV and projecting number of subscribers as well as components of CLV in the future.

Finally, a focus on CLV also has implications for how finance executives view marketing spending. Traditionally, marketing spending has been expensed whereas, say, R&D has been treated as investments. Given that marketing dollars spent to acquire or retain customers enhance their CLV, which in turn influences firm and shareholder value, many marketing expenditures should be logically treated as investments as well. Put differently, money spent acquiring customers to grow "organically" is as much an investment as is the money spent to acquire a company in order to gain access to its customers, and probably less risky than investments in basic R&D.

Implications for Marketing Educators

The focus on CLV represents a step in the gradual evolution of marketing from a focus on the present and the product to one on the future and the customer. In its earliest form, marketing involved transportation, i.e., getting products to the marketplace. In essence the value of CLV was treated as zero. In its next phase, marketing focused on sales, i.e., moving the units it took to the market. In this era, CLV was effectively equivalent to current sales. Following this, "modern" marketing began to take hold. Here focus was on the 4 P's and then STP (segmenting, targeting, and positioning). The importance of share began to be emphasized. Since share is determined by the number of customers (i.e., acquisition and retention) times the volume per customer (i.e., expansion), it incorporated key elements of CLV and was viewed as a key to profit (Buzzell and Gale 1987). More recently, customers as long-term assets have been emphasized so that CLV, along with customer experience and customer relationships, have become central constructs. This change in emphasis (and attendant metrics) has a direct impact on managerial decisions and the way we teach marketing in the classroom.

While just about every marketing course emphasizes the importance of the customer, traditional 4 P, STP-based courses viewed customers essentially as constraints on their actions. "Know your customers" essentially translated into know enough about your customers so that your tactics (e.g., cent off promotion, ad copy) are effective.

Contrast to this the implicit focus of customer centricity, customer experience management or relationship marketing. The mantras "the customer is king," "delight the customer," etc. tip the scales from a focus on the company to a focus on the customer with the implicit assumption (hope?) that pleasing the customer guarantees profits. (A simple counter example: a price of zero and/or infinite quality pleases the customer but bankrupts the company).

Interestingly, CLV may engender a more balanced perspective. By focusing on the customer, it maintains an external perspective. However, by emphasizing net revenue, it also focuses on the value of the customer to the company.

Consider the basic ("core") marketing course. Using CLV as an organizing construct has three main impacts. First, it makes the course more quantitative. Ironically, this appeals to non-marketing majors (e.g., those in finance who make up the majority of students) more than many of those in marketing (who are happy talking about ad copy and relationships). Second, it deemphasizes the 4 P's in general and advertising in particular. Third, it gives marketing a more long-run and strategic orien-. tation. The criterion for evaluation (CLV) is inherently future oriented. Therefore, actions are considered in terms of their impact on, say, acquisition, retention, and expansion rather than same period sales or profits.

LIMITATIONS AND FUTURE RESEARCH

No concept is a panacea and this is true for CLV as well. This metric is most suitable for customer or subscriber-based businesses (e.g., telecoms, magazine subscriptions, cable, internet firms, financial services such as credit card, etc.). It is less clear how the concept applies to businesses such as pharmaceutical (where R&D is critical) or oil drilling.

For many fast-growing companies (e.g., Google) a large portion of the value is in the "option value." In other words, a large customer base gives these companies an option to go into many different businesses in the future via expansion. Current models of CLV do not capture this option value. In fact, we may even wish to consider a customer as a "real option" where a manager may decide to invest more or less in a customer depending on his/her future response to marketing actions. The large finance literature on real options may be useful for developing such models.

Another key aspect missing from current CLV models is network effects. Current models of CLV consider a customer in isolation. However, the emergence of network-based communities, such as myspace.com, and the increasing importance of buzz-marketing highlights the importance of word-of-mouth and customer networks. In their study, Gupta et al. (2004) found that their estimates of customer value were far below the market value of eBay. They hypothesized that part of the reason for this discrepancy was that they did not capture network effects.

CONCLUSION

The basic premise of this paper is that the concept of CLV is central to multiple constituencies. As such, it provides a common focus (and metric) for cross-functional decision-making and conversation. Further and importantly, it also provides a basis for valuing companies and assessing various stocks.

Relations among the various business functions tend to be uneasy at best and sometimes antagonistic. One reason for this is the non-intersection of goals (metrics). For example, marketing focuses on awareness and attitude, operations on capacity utilization and defect rates, R&D on the number of new products developed and their cycle time (speed to market), and finance on return on capital and P/E ratios. Small wonder, then, that these distinct goals and the different languages they spawn create confusion and misunderstanding.

This paper takes the position that CLV provides a bridge between functional areas. In particular, it argues that CLV is both the culmination of marketing efforts (and outside influences) and the future revenue stream which determines firm value. Further, because it is based on some simple and explicit assumptions about the future (i.e., acquisition, retention, and expansion rates and costs), it is relatively easy both to measure it and to critically evaluate its level and its components.

The paper explicitly addresses how to assess acquisition, retention, and expansion. It also demonstrates how their combination (CLV) can be used as a measure of the value of a business. Examples demonstrate close equivalence of total CLV and financial market value in several cases. The differences that arise (e.g., for eBay and Amazon) suggest possible modifications to the metric (e.g., accounting for network effects and option value). The methods suggested are relatively simple conceptually (although making precise assumptions is a chancy activity at best). The real power of the concept, however, may extend well beyond measurement and valuation. Indeed, its power may be in laying the groundwork for a "unified theory" of marketing which is relevant and understandable both inside and outside the marketing function.

NOTES

1. All financial information is obtained from the investor reports available at *www.netflix.com* . Market value and stock price numbers were obtained from Yahoo Finance, *http://finance.yahoo.com*

2. We have excluded other fixed costs such as administrative costs. In 2003, Netflix reported its subscribers' CLV where they showed that these costs are almost equal to the depreciation and amortization that are added back to arrive at EBITDA.

REFERENCES

Bass, Frank (1969), "A New Product Growth Model for Consumer Durables," *Management Science,* 15(5), 215-27.

Bitran, Gabriel and Susana Mondschein (1996), "Mailing Decisions in the Catalog Sales Industry," *Management Science,* 42(9).

Blattberg, Robert, Gary Getz and Jacquelyn S. Thomas (2001), *Customer Equity: Building and Managing Relationships as Valuable Assets.* Boston, MA. Harvard Business School Press.

Bolton, Ruth N. (1998), "A Dynamic Model of the Duration of the Customer's Relationship with a Continuous Service Provider: The Role of Satisfaction," *Marketing Science*, 17(1), 46-65.

Brealey, Richard A. and Stewart C. Myers (1996), *Principles of Corporate Finance*, 5th Edition. New York: McGraw Hills.

Damodaran, Aswath (2001), *The Dark Side of Valuation: Valuing Old Tech, New Tech, and New Economy Companies*. Prentice Hall.

Demers, Elizabeth and Baruch Lev (2001), "A Rude Awakening: Internet Shakeout in 2000," *Review of Accounting Studies*, 6, 2/3, 331-359.

Desmet, Driek, Tracy Francis, Alice Hu, Timothy M. Koller, and George A. Riedel (2000), "Valuing Dot-coms," *McKinsey Quarterly*, 1, 148-157.

Fader, Peter, Bruce Hardie and Ka Lok Lee (2005), "RFM and CLV: Using Iso-CLV Curves for Customer Base Analysis," *Journal of Marketing Research*, XLII (November), 415-430.

Fisher, J.C. and R.H. Pry (1971), "A Simple Substitution Model for Technology Change," *Technological Forecasting and Social Change*, 3, 75-88.

Gonul, Fusun, Byung-Do Kim and Mengze Shi (2000), "Mailing Smarter to Catalog Customers," *Journal of Interactive Marketing*, 14 (2), 2-16.

Gupta, Sunil and Donald R. Lehmann (2003), "Customers as Assets," *Journal of Interactive Marketing*, 17(1), Winter, 9-24.

Gupta, Sunil and Donald R. Lehmann (2005), *Managing Customers as Investments*. Philadelphia, PA: Wharton School Publishing.

Gupta, Sunil, Donald R. Lehmann and Jennifer Ames Stuart (2004), "Valuing Customers," *Journal of Marketing Research*, 41(1), February, 7-18.

Gupta, Sunil and Valarie Zeithaml (2006), "Customer Metrics and Their Impact on Financial Performance," *Working Paper*, Columbia University.

Gupta, Sunil, Dominique Hanssens, Bruce Hardie, Wiliam Kahn, V. Kumar, Nathaniel Lin, Nalini Ravishankar and S. Sriram (2006), "Modeling Customer Lifetime Value," *Journal of Service Research*, forthcoming.

Jedidi, Kamel, Carl Mela and Sunil Gupta (1999), "Managing Advertising and Promotion for Long-Run Profitability," *Marketing Science*, 18(1), 1-22.

Kim, Namwoon, Vijay Mahajan and Rajendra K. Srivastava (1995), "Determining the Going Market Value of a Business in an Emerging Information Technology Industry: The Case of the Cellular Communications Industry," *Technological Forecasting and Social Change*, 49, 257-279.

Knott, Aaron, Andrew Hayes and Scott Neslin (2002), "Next-Product-to-Buy Models for Cross-Selling Applications," *Journal of Interactive Marketing*, 16(3), 59-75.

Libai, Barak, Eitan Muller and Renana Peres (2006), "The Diffusion of Services," *Working Paper*, Tel Aviv University.

Mela, Carl, Sunil Gupta and Donald R. Lehmann (1997), "The Long-Term Impact of Promotion and Advertising on Consumer Brand Choice," *Journal of Marketing Research*, 34 (May), 248-261.

Neslin, Scott, Sunil Gupta, Wagner Kamakura, Junxiang Lu and Charlotte Mason (2006), "Defection Detection: Measuring and Understanding the Predictive Accuracy of Customer Churn Models," *Journal of Marketing Research*, forthcoming.

Pfeifer, Phillip and Robert Carraway (2000), "Modeling Customer Relationships as Markov Chains," *Journal of Interactive Marketing*, 14(2), 43-55.

Reinartz, Werner and V. Kumar (2000), "On the Profitability of Long-life Customers in a Noncontractual Setting: An Empirical Investigation and Implications for Marketing", *Journal of Marketing*, 64, (October), 17-35.

Reinartz, Werner and V. Kumar (2003), "The Impact of Customer Relationship Characteristics on Profitable Lifetime Duration," *Journal of Marketing*, 67(1), January, 77-99.

Reinartz, Werner, Jacquelyn Thomas and V. Kumar (2005), "Balancing Acquisition and Retention Resources to Maximize Customer Profitability," *Journal of Marketing*, 69(1), January, 63-79.

Rust, Roland, Valarie Zeithaml and Katherine Lemon (2000), *Driving Customer Equity* New York: Free Press.

Schmittlein, David C., Donald G. Morrison, and Richard Colombo (1987), "Counting Your Customers: Who They Are and What Will They Do Next?" *Management Science*, 33 (January), 1-24.

Thomas, Jacquelyn (2001), "A Methodology for Linking Customer Acquisition to Customer Retention," *Journal of Marketing Research*, 38(2), May, 262-268.

Trueman, Brett, M.H. Franco Wong and Xiao-Jun Zhang (2001), "The Eyeballs Have It: Searching for the Value in Internet Stocks," *Review of Accounting Studies*, Supplement.

Venkatesan, Rajkumar and V. Kumar (2004), "A Customer Lifetime Value Framework for Customer Selection and Resource Allocation Strategy," *Journal of Marketing*, 68(4), 106-125.

Verhoef, Peter, Philip Franses and Janny Hoekstra (2001), "The Impact of Satisfaction and Payment Equity on Cross -Buying: A Dynamic Model for a Multi-Service Provider," *Journal of Retailing*, 77(3), 359-378.

doi:10.1300/J366v05n02_06

The Climate for Service:
A Review of the Construct
with Implications for Achieving CLV Goals

Benjamin Schneider

Valtera Corporation

William H. Macey

Valtera Corporation

Scott A. Young

Valtera Corporation

SUMMARY. We develop a framework in which internal employees'
diagnoses of their firm's service climate determine their role behavior
towards customers and, ultimately, customer satisfaction, loyalty, retention and shareholder value. Elements of the framework include: (1) foun-

Benjamin Schneider, PhD, is Senior Research Fellow, Valtera Corporation, and
Professor Emeritus, University of Maryland.

William H. Macey, PhD, is CEO, Valtera Corporation, 1701 Golf Road, Tower 2,
Suite 1100, Rolling Meadows, IL 60008 (E-mail: WMacey@valtera.com).

Scott A. Young, PhD, is Managing Consultant, Valtera Corporation, 1701 Golf
Road, Tower 2, Suite 1100, Rolling Meadows, IL 60008 (E-mail: syoung@valtera.
com).

Address correspondence to: Benjamin Schneider, Valtera Corporation, 1363 Caminito
Floreo, Suite G, La Jolla, CA 92037 (E-mail: bschneider@valtera.com).

[Haworth co-indexing entry note]: "The Climate for Service: A Review of the Construct with Implications for Achieving CLV Goals." Schneider, Benjamin, William H. Macey, and Scott A. Young. Co-published simultaneously in *Journal of Relationship Marketing* (Best Business Books, an imprint of The
Haworth Press, Inc.) Vol. 5, No. 2/3, 2006, pp. 111-132; and: *Customer Lifetime Value: Reshaping the Way
We Manage to Maximize Profits* (ed: David Bejou, Timothy L. Keiningham, and Lerzan Aksoy) Best Business Books, an imprint of The Haworth Press, Inc., 2006, pp. 111-132. Single or multiple copies of this article
are available for a fee from The Haworth Document Delivery Service [1-800-HAWORTH, 9:00 a.m. - 5:00
p.m. (EST). E-mail address: docdelivery@haworthpress.com].

111

dation issues (fundamental human behavior issues like the presence of necessary resources and the quality of leadership), (2) internal service (the quality of service employees report they receive internally from others), (3) service climate (the degree to which management emphasizes service quality in all of its activities), and (4) customer-focused service behavior. How this research is done is reviewed and research supporting elements of the framework is described. How the approach can be adapted for promoting CLV goals is explicated and answers to some frequently asked questions about change to an organization with a service quality and CLV focus are described. *doi:10.1300/J366v05n02_07 [Article copies available for a fee from The Haworth Document Delivery Service: 1-800-HAWORTH. E-mail address: <docdelivery@haworthpress.com> Website: <http://www.HaworthPress.com> © 2006 by The Haworth Press, Inc. All rights reserved.]*

KEYWORDS. Customer lifetime value, strategic management, objectives, human resource management, organizational behavior, financial performance

There are two major elements to our thesis. First, the operating environment employees experience determines their behavior. Second, the behavior of employees extends beyond organizational boundaries by how they directly or indirectly create customer experiences, especially in face-to-face service enterprises. In more crude terminology, ya can't hide what happens inside the organization from the outside world. We agree with Bund (2006) who argues that organizations have been designed to focus on internal organizational processes without much regard for the external world the organizations are designed to serve. She argues for the outside-in organization which for her means starting with customers and aligning the organization so that it focuses on them and not on what looks and feels good internally. She and we agree. We see that the major challenge of the management of organizations is to choose the strategic goals they want to achieve and then align the internal organization with those goals so they are achievable.

Our view is that too many organizations choose strategic goals and then wish for them to be achieved rather than implementing the tactics required to achieve them. How can they know if they are engaging in wishful thinking or are actually implementing the tactics likely to achieve their goals? They must monitor what is happening where the rubber meets the road. In service organizations this means they must monitor the degree to which the strategic goal, say a focus on customer lifetime value (CLV), is being implemented in the daily life of the employees of the organization. What we now know, and as we will document in what follows, is that employee observations on the degree to which a strategic focus is being implemented is significantly related to goal accomplishment. The evidence is particularly strong for employee observations of the service climate in which they work and the goals of customer satisfaction, retention and loyalty (Schneider & White, 2004)–key components of CLV. We focus on CLV as a strategic goal, but our logic applies to other strategic goals as well. Zohar (2000) provides an example of similar reasoning regarding safety at work.

Our impression is that marketers have perhaps overly focused on the outside customer and have largely ignored the importance of the internal organization for meeting customer goals. Thus, we view the focus on the customer and his or her satisfaction, retention and loyalty as a challenge to be met by aligning the internal organization to achieve those goals.

The evidence accumulating on this linkage between internal organizational design and customer satisfaction, retention and loyalty is quite robust. In businesses as diverse as banks, insurance companies, auto dealerships, hotels, truck rental, R & D, and consulting, a variation on the same theme emerges: Employee descriptions of the way their organizations function vis-à-vis service and customer focus are significantly correlated with customer experiences (Bowen & Ford, 2002; Dean, 2004; Ryan & Ployhart, 2003; Schneider & White, 2004). When employees describe their organization as one that rewards, supports, and expects excellence in service quality and/or has a strong customer orientation, customers of those same organizations report they receive superior service and/or are satisfied–and that they will be loyal to the firm (Heskett, Sasser & Schlesinger, 1997; Schneider, Ashworth, Higgs & Carr, 1996; Schneider, White & Paul, 1998). It appears to be true that (a) employees are accurate diagnosticians of how well the internal organization is functioning against strategic goals, (b) employees who work in organizations that are actually implementing a customer-focused strategy extend themselves to service customers well, and (c) this yields increased levels of customer satisfaction and loyalty.

In what follows, we first consider some basic observations about humans as social beings because this is a root cause of the linkage discovered between employee and customer experiences. Second, we introduce the organizational behavior construct of organizational climate that serves as the organizing theme for how both employees and customers experience their organizations. Then we review the approach characterized in the research literatures revealing the connection between internal service climate and external customer satisfaction, retention and loyalty–those facets of customer experiences and behavior that finally eventuate in CLV. We summarize the presentation by arguing that in order to achieve a CLV focus, firms must take a multi-pronged approach to strategy implementation or the entire attempt will fail. Finally, we present answers to a set of questions we are frequently asked about changing an organization to a service climate to achieve these important customer-centric goals.

ON UNDERSTANDING RELATIONSHIPS IN SERVICE FIRMS

Humans are social animals and when they interact with others they attempt for the most part to be agreeable, positive, and in other ways interpersonally sensitive and competent. The personality psychologist Hogan (1996) calls this the inclination to get along. He argues that the inclination to get along is part of everyday life–and that includes work life as well: "What goes on at work is formally identical to what goes on in life; any distinction between organizational behavior and social behavior in general is artificial" (Hogan, 2004, p. 13). We extend this logic to suggest that relationships at work are not limited to relationships with coworkers but to relationships with all people with whom one comes in contact–like customers, for example. While the notion of people as social beings has been invoked in the relationship marketing literature (e.g., Morgan, 2000; Sheth & Parvatiyar, 1995), this has typically been true from the vantage point of customers' experiences and the consequences of those experiences, and less so from the organizational behavior side.

When we hear the term "organizational behavior" the image that comes to mind is of a firm doing something. But firms do nothing; it is the people in them who do things (Schneider, 1987). If it is people who do things in organizations, then the critical issue requiring attention for our understanding of the creation and maintenance of a customer-centric organization (Bund, 2006) is to ask what drives the behavior of people in life and at work. Lewin (1935) many years ago proposed that it is a combination of the personal attributes of people and the environments ("life space") in which they exist that jointly determines their behavior. If the behavior of interest is the social behavior between server and served, then we must look to the personal attributes of people who serve and the environmental characteristics in which they work to understand ways to enhance the relationship experiences of customers.

In the present paper, we will deal almost exclusively with issues concerning the environment that firms must create if the behavior they want from employees is focused on relationship-building with customers. There already is good evidence that interpersonally- and service-oriented people can be hired for service (Hogan, Hogan & Busch, 1984) and sales jobs (Michaels & Day, 1985). Frei and McDaniel (1998), for example, presented a meta-analysis of 41 validity studies of various service orientation personality measures and showed consistent relationships between these measures and actual job performance of service workers. In-depth analyses of these 41 studies revealed that the personality attributes that were most predictive of supervisory ratings of the job performance of service workers were Agreeableness, Emotional Stability (sometimes labeled by its opposite, Neuroticism) and Conscientiousness; see Table 2 in Frei & McDaniel, 1998). These personality facets are from the so-called Five Factor Model (FFM) of personality, the dimensional framework most often used in contemporary research on personality in the workplace (see Barrick & Mount, 1991). But once hired, the fact is that even service-oriented people vary in the level of service behavior they display to customers as a function of the kind of messages they receive about what is important in that environment. Our task here is to focus on that environment because it is the environment of the service facility with which the customer comes in contact. We conceptualize environments in psychological terms and use the construct of organizational climate as our organizing theme.

ORGANIZATIONAL CLIMATE

Organizational behavior scientists either implicitly or explicitly believe that observed human behavior in a setting is a function of the salience or meaning of the setting for the people there. Except for extreme behaviorists, behavior is conceptualized as the outcome of a sense-making process wherein the activities and events experienced are processed by humans who then behave as a function of the meaning they attach to what they experience (Weick, 1995). Organizational climate scholars have been concerned with how this sense-making–filtering, processing, and the attaching of meaning–in and to organizations happens, and the consequences associated with this process (James, James, & Asch, 1990).

As noted earlier, Lewin (1935) called this notion of the experienced situation the "life space." By "life space" he meant the total situation as experienced by individuals. Indeed, Lewin, Lippitt, and White (1939) are the first to use the term "climate" in the sense we are using it here: a shared perception of the atmosphere, tone or mood of a setting combined with the behavior characteristic of that setting. When people in a setting come to share the meaning of a situation we may assume that what they share is as much a property of the organization as any other facet of it (Schneider, 2000).

Lewin et al's. explication of climate resulted in numerous efforts by psychological researchers to design survey-based measures of climate, measures designed to capture the activities, events, and behaviors that characterized settings. As research accumulated, the number of dimensions of climate that emerged proliferated making it difficult to identify what "climate" was being assessed in any research effort. Schneider (1975) argued that climate, to be useful, had to be strategically focused–a climate *for something* like service or safety or innovation. For example, there is good evidence now to support the idea that the service climate experienced by employees in organizations is shared also by the customers those employees serve (cf. Schneider et al., 1998); one might even say there is a shared climate for *parties* to an organization, not just the *members* of an organization.

It is useful to take a brief side road here to note that there is a similar construct in the organizational behavior literature to the one we have been discussing; it is called organizational culture. Research on organizational culture tends to focus less on activities, events, and behavior and more on shared values, myths, stories, and beliefs that characterize organizational members and thus the organizations of which they are members (Martin, 2002; Schein, 2000). For an extended discussion of climate and culture see Ashkanasy, Wilderom, and Peterson (2000). In the present paper, we focus on the survey work related to a specific form of organizational climate, the climate for service. We formally define climate as the meaning attached to the focus of events, practices and procedures and the behavior that gets rewarded, supported and expected in a setting (Schneider, 1975).

We focus on climate because it captures the information processing people do of the various stimuli they encounter at work. Climate refers to the meaning people in a work environment attach to the cues they perceive about the required foci of their energies and competencies. The climate of an organization is a summary impression employees have about "how we do things around here" or "what we focus on around here" or "what we direct our efforts to around here." Climate provides a psychological identity of an organization for employees and the typical finding is that employees in a work environment (especially in an interdependent work environment) come to share this common identity. The identity might be that "we do service here" or "service quality is the watchword here." The common identity can be less positive–or even negative–and thus might be something other than service quality. In one project, we had employees in an organization describe the service orientation of the firm this way: "Our approach to service is to consider the customer guilty until proven innocent" (Schneider, Wheeler & Cox, 1992). To the degree that the identity employees ascribe to the organization is aligned with the desired service quality, employees will be active contributors to these strategic goals. The point is that such foci for employee behavior do not emerge unless employees are surrounded with meaningful activities–cues and clues–that service quality is the way business is done.

In what follows we describe several projects in which we and others have documented this linkage between internal service climate and external customer satisfaction and loyalty. Then we provide a framework that has emerged from this work for understanding how to build a service climate–a climate that will yield, through the behavior of employees, the important outcomes we have noted.

LINKING INTERNAL AND EXTERNAL WORLDS: THE APPROACH

These projects have been characterized by the integration of organizational behavior diagnostic survey data and marketing data vis-à-vis customer service quality experiences, customer satisfaction, and customer intentions. The general approach has been to conduct focus groups with employees to identify the service climate of the organization and the events, practices and behavior they and other employees experience that constitute their climate perceptions. For example, employees may note in response to a query about the kind of climate that characterizes their workplace that "This is a really service-oriented company." This kind of comment will be followed up by questions from the focus group leader like "What kinds of things do you see happening that make you feel that way?" This question elicits the specific activities that constitute a service-oriented climate. As another example of what makes for such a climate, focus group members may note that their manager plans for, sets goals for, and recognizes excellent service. Or, they may note that they have the resources (equipment, training, staffing levels) they need to serve customers and that they take action on customer feedback so that problems do not recur. Or, less obviously, that the marketing department ensures that the systems are in place to deliver a new offering prior to releasing the advertisements for that new offering to the news media. The point is to illuminate the routines and behaviors that send messages to employees about service quality and to which they attach meaning with regard to service excellence.

The focus groups identify not only events, practices and procedures and the behaviors that get rewarded, supported, and expected vis-à-vis service; they also report on more generic management approaches of the organization. For example, in response to the question about the climate of the organization, focus group members might reply: "We treat the customers fairly because that is the way we are treated." The issue of fairness can then be pursued further both with regard to the specifics of fair treatment of customers and fair treatment of employees. We have learned that fairness has very complex underpinnings for people (employees and customers, too; Tax & Brown, 2000) and that feelings of fair treatment are central to trust–and that trust is central to the establishment and maintenance of a relationship–with employees and with customers, too (Bowen, Gilliland & Folger, 1999).

The specific behaviors, practices and events that emerge from the focus groups are turned into survey items for administration to employees across the service units of a business (e.g., bank branches for banks, real estate agencies for real estate companies, insurance agencies for insurance companies, and so forth). These units are chosen because they then become the units of analysis for the research effort across which the linkage between employee and customer data is established.

Service Climate Survey Content

In our more recent work, the employee surveys based on many focus groups (Schneider et al., 1992) have four major components to them. The first component we refer to as "foundation issues." These are fundamental human resources issues having to do with fairness and trust (participation in decision-making, availability of information), the availability of resources (training, equipment, technology, facilities, systems), and general management/leadership practices as employees experience them (responsive, helpful). The concern with the foundation issues is captured by the saying "House built on a weak foundation will not last for long, oh no." Our experience reveals that attempting to create and maintain a service climate on a foundation of poor human resources management practices will likely be futile. Importantly, we do not claim that the positive human resources practices associated with the foundation issues *make* or *cause* a service climate; we claim they provide a foundation on which a service climate can be built (Schneider et al., 1998).

The second section of the survey includes items devoted to "internal service." Internal service concerns how employees in an organization describe the service they receive internally from others on whom they depend (Reynoso & Moores, 1995). Issues such as the cooperativeness of others, the responsiveness of others, the competencies of others, and so forth, are assessed with regard to "the other group inside the business on whom your work most depends." We have found that the higher the level of internal service delivery reported in a unit (branch, agency), the more positive customer reports are with respect to service quality. In one project, for example, we showed that branch bank reports from employees on the internal service they received significantly predicted customer satisfaction (Schneider et al., 1998).

The third section of the survey focuses specifically on the kinds of clues and cues employees observe happening around them vis-à-vis the focus on service quality. Items on this part of the survey explicitly concern service quality and address such issues as: (a) management's reinforcement and recognition of service excellence, (b) management's planning for and setting goals for service quality, (c) the competencies of other employees to deliver service quality, (d) the availability of the necessary tools, equipment and resources to deliver service, and (e) the attention paid to customer feedback on service quality. Note that the items assessing the presence of these features of the workplace all refer to them in terms of service quality. Thus, the questions do not ask about the presence of rewards and recognition but the presence of those for service excellence; similarly, the items do not ask about the degree to which coworkers are competent, but the degree to which coworkers are competent to deliver service quality. As another example, note that the presence of tools and equipment appears both as a foundation issue and as a service climate issue. In the former case such presence refers to generic tools and equipment while in the latter case it refers specifically to those required for delivering service quality. It is the focus on service quality that makes for a positive service climate. This particular set of issues targeted on service delivery has emerged over time as the "bundle" or "cluster" of issues that define, in the aggregate, a service climate (see also Lytle, Hom & Mokwa, 1998).

The fourth area that the surveys cover concerns the behavior on the part of employees that yields customer satisfaction. In recent work, it has been shown that it is not just service climate that gets reflected in customer satisfaction and loyalty but that it is service climate that results in customer-focused behavior, and it is this behavior that yields customer satisfaction which, in turn, yields sales (Bettencourt & Brown, 1997; Schneider, Ehrhart, Mayer, Saltz & Niles-Jolly, 2005).

For the development of a service climate survey focused specifically on a climate in which CLV strategic goals have been set, focus group participants might be asked to elaborate on such issues as the degree to which:

- Specific goals exist for CLV achievements
- Measurement systems have been designed to provide continuous information on goal achievement to unit (branch, agency) employees
- Recognition and reward systems have been tied to achieving CLV goals
- Technology points out to employees the value of customers when their names or other identifiers are entered as part of a service encounter
- Training has been received on precisely what CLV is, how it is calculated, and what its component causes are (customer satisfaction, customer retention, and so forth)
- The unit manager "walks the CLV talk" by discussing CLV of customers in training, meetings, performance appraisals, and so forth
- The unit manager has been trained to educate and train employees on what CLV is, how important it is for the long-term growth of the business, and so forth
- Newcomers to the unit are imbued with the CLV concept and practices.

Our underlying belief is that just as a service climate must be built on a strong HR foundation, a focus on CLV can only be built on a positive service climate; CLV cannot exist in a vacuum.

On the Links Between Service Climate and Customer Satisfaction . . . and Beyond

Our research, and increasingly the research of others, shows that when *employees* report the presence of strong human resources foundation issues, excellent internal service, a strong positive service climate, and high levels of customer-focused behavior, then *customers* report excellent service quality, high customer satisfaction, strong intentions to maintain and renew their business with the target firm, and strong intentions to recommend the business to others (Bowen & Ford, 2002; Dean, 2004; Schneider et al., 1996; Wiley, 1996). These results extend out significantly in time with service climate predicting customer experiences three years later in one project (Schneider et al., 1998). Dean's (2004, p. 345) review of the research crossing organizational diagnoses against customer outcomes has the following conclusion: "The most compelling evidence links organizational features, employee attitudes, service quality, customer responses and financial outcomes."

Recent evidence on the link between customer satisfaction and financial outcomes has been particularly impressive and there is no reason to suspect that this relationship would be any different for CLV as the outcome of interest. While we have known for some time that service quality yields customer satisfaction and improvements in accounting-based ratio measures of firm performance like ROI (Zahorik & Rust, 1992) and that customer satisfaction is a key to customer loyalty (Reichheld, 1996), the connections to the future value of the firm have been more difficult to show–until recently. Anderson, Fornell and Mazvancheryl (2004), using the American Customer Satisfaction Index (ACSI) as the driver, showed that customer satisfaction at the organizational level of analysis significantly predicts shareholder value using Tobin's q (1969). Tobin's q is a ratio of a firm's market value to the current replacement costs of its assets. A follow-up study by Gruca and Rego (2005) reveals some of the intermediate linkages in the relationship between the ACSI and shareholder value. That is, in a longitudinal study they showed that satisfaction predicts firms' increasing future cash flow growth and reduces variability in such growth, both of which predict shareholder value.

In our own research we have recently studied the internal-external relationship between service climate and the ACSI and, as in the research reviewed earlier, show significant relationships between service climate and the ACSI as well as significant relationships between customer-focused behavior on the part of employees and the ACSI (Macey

& Schneider, in press; Schneider, Macey, Young, & Lee, 2006). These results, when combined with the Anderson et al. (2004) and Gruca and Rego (2005) findings and those reviewed earlier, suggest a long-linked model as shown in Figure 1 between internal organizational processes and financial outcomes of importance to organizations.

A number of features of Figure 1 require some commentary. First, the figure begins with the foundation issues discussed earlier. In essence, the argument is that if the organization is not well-managed to begin with, then building a service climate is not likely. It is a service climate that is required for an organization to actually achieve the behaviors towards customers designed to increase the customer satisfaction and loyalty that optimize CLV. In short, marketing professionals must align with HR to ensure that fundamental issues in the management of service employees are attended to in ways that promote the strong foundation on which a service climate can be built. Indeed, there is research to show that when employees work in an organization with a strong HR

FIGURE 1. A Framework for Understanding the Organizational Conditions That Lead to a Focus on Customer Lifetime Value

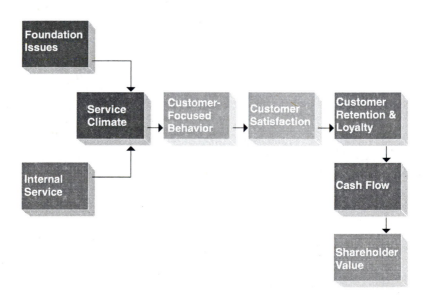

foundation they become attitudinally engaged, and it is when employees are attitudinally engaged that the service climate in which they work eventuates in customer satisfaction and loyalty (Salanova & Peiro, in press).

Second, as a long-linked model, one would not expect a direct relationship between the foundation issues and/or internal service, for example, to be significantly related to market value. It is what foundation issues provide a basis for, the creation of a service climate, that yields the behavior that in turn creates customer satisfaction and the desirable financial outcomes that follow. Service climate might not even be directly related to market value because of the numerous intermediate links identified in Figure 1 between it and market value. Our caution, then is that changes in foundation issues or internal service might not be immediately reflected in market value but will likely appear over time as they work their way through the various links in Figure 1. The first significant implication of this is that the issue of proximal (nearby in time) and distal (further removed in time) effects must be a conscious part of both planning and setting expectations when attempting to improve customer satisfaction and indeed financial consequences like market value (Schneider et al., 2006). Too many managers have a "light switch" mentality when it comes to organizational change, believing that you turn on foundation issues (for example) and you immediately achieve improvements in market value. Organizations, made up of humans who are *appropriately* slow to change (we only want them to change when *we* want them to change!), take time to react and that is why it is so critically important to ensure that everything possible is done to promote the service climate focus. Coffee mugs and posters do not a service climate make. Service climate requires attention to the many issues noted earlier (rewards and recognition for service excellence, planning for and setting service goals, providing the human and technological resources required to produce service quality, attending to customer feedback with action, and so forth).

The second important implication of the time lag between links in the model is that employees observe, and if asked will report, negative changes in the service climate long before those changes produce corresponding decreases in customer or financial metrics. Therefore, the company that detects service issues via service climate data will be able to intervene, correct problems, and reap the benefits much sooner than its competitor who investigates and addresses the problem only in response to a drop in customer satisfaction or loyalty. In other words, if over time a company is able to consistently detect and correct problems faster than the competition, it should gain increasing competitive advantage.

Third, on this last thought, one may ask: Whose responsibility is it to make these things happen? Our work (Schneider et al., 2006) and the work of others (Buckingham & Coffman, 1999) reveal that the local unit leader is the person who makes the local climate to which employees respond. We have deduced the importance of what we call "service leadership," activities focused on the creation and maintenance of a service climate. Everything the local leader does is observed and the cumulation of the local leaders' choices about how they spend their time, and on what they focus their energies, sends the most powerful messages about what is important in and to the unit. In one set of focus groups we have recently run, we asked the question: How do you know what to do when confronted with a situation with customers you may not have encountered before? The answer: We ask ourselves what would the manager do? Unit leader/first-line supervisor jobs are first and foremost role models. They are not only leaders but they are doers and it is what they promote through their leadership and what they display as doers that help create the local service climate.

Of course, this makes the selection, training, and support of the unit manager a higher-level management responsibility. These local managers can only provide the resources that they in turn have been given; they can only ensure internal service to their unit and to other units if management ensures that the staff functions on whom unit managers depend provide them with what they need. We've worked in banks, for example, where marketing people design new offerings and then get so excited by the possibilities that they advertise them before the branches are trained to deliver them (Schneider & Bowen, 1985). In another system, a mortgage bank, regional managers encouraged local branch managers to delay replacing receptionists to save costs so their profits would look better; now that is a truly service-oriented ploy! The point is that just as unit employees model their local manager, the local manager will model those above the unit level. It is at higher levels where strategy emerges, and it is at those higher levels where actions must begin that reveal through daily decisions and behavior that the new strategy is going to be implemented and not just be the flavor of the month (Burke, 2003).

Hidden in Figure 1 and our discussion to date of service climate, so we wish to make it explicit, is the fact that employee observations of the service quality focus of their organization–observations on the degree to which strategic goals are actually being implemented in the local unit–are significantly reflected in customer satisfaction, a leading indicator of shareholder value. The idea that employees are valuable and accurate reporters of internal policies and practices, including strategy implementation, is central to the philosophy underlying our work. That is, the research proceeds from the vantage point that those who deliver service to customers know best the degree to which strategy is actually being implemented including what happens to facilitate and support, or denigrate and restrict, service quality for customers; which in turn yields cash flow and increased shareholder value. Based on the strength and robustness of these findings it can no longer be thought that employees' observations of their organization are nice to know but not strategically useful. Employees not only deliver the service that yields customer satisfaction, with its known consequences, but they can identify the ways the organization can function more effectively in creating the planned-for customer experiences. It is obvious by now that here we are not describing results for typical employee attitude or opinion surveys, but surveys targeted on the strategic behavior of organizations and their members (Macey & Schneider, in press).

SUMMATION AND CONCLUDING THOUGHTS: THE THREE-LEGGED STOOL

If an organization desires to achieve a service climate that will eventuate in an increased focus on CLV with its attendant financial consequences, there are a number of avenues to take. One avenue is to focus on the core aspect of the service—the comprehensiveness of the offering (e.g., comprehensiveness of the insurance policies), the inherent quality of the offering (food in a restaurant, clothing in a retail store, the bed in a hotel room), and so forth. We have not discussed these core attributes of the offering here because our focus was on the less tangible HR/OB issues connected with the *delivery* of the offering. However, these core attributes of the offering are ignored at the organization's peril (see Grönroos, 1990, for explication of the role of the core service). A second avenue to success is to focus on marketing the advantages of the firm's core offerings; this is also very critical because if people are not aware of the offering they will not purchase it. The third avenue, and the one addressed in this brief article, is to focus on the internal organization and its human resources as another vehicle for providing the level of customer satisfaction required for eventual firm success.

We now think of service organization success as being built on a three-legged stool. One leg is the attributes of the core offering. A second leg is the marketing of the core attributes. And the third leg concerns the management of the internal organization. If any of those legs is not attended to, the stool falls. All legs must be functional, attended to, and nurtured for a company to actualize a strategy.

Organizational effectiveness, then, is an outcome of at least product design, marketing, and organizational design all aligned to support the strategic positioning, if you will, of the brand. Brands do not have to have the "finest" brand image; they need to have a positive and distinctive brand image. In the world of service, all organizations do not have to deliver the "finest" service quality to have a distinctive brand image. For example, McDonald's has a specific brand image that connotes reliability, consistency, cleanliness and fun–it is not Chez Francois but it is distinctive and successful. The climate created at McDonald's for employees is one in which employees are provided a realistic preview of the job and then they encounter a fair, carefully defined and controlled workplace requiring exquisite teamwork; McDonald's has been successful attracting potential employees who fit its needs. At McDonald's, both employees and customers have clear sets of expectations and the challenge is to deliver against both–and then the relationship between the two can exist and flourish. The core, the marketing, and the organizational design, in alignment, optimize the achievement of strategic goals.

We believe that the core offering and the marketing legs of the stool have received more attention in the thinking about customer satisfaction and its consequences than has the organizational design and the management of human resources (Lovelock & Wirtz, 2005; Schneider & Bowen, 1995; Schneider & White, 2004). Especially in the world of services, this is shortsighted because the world of consumer services is one in which the relationship between consumer and service deliverer will be relatively intimate–it is both psychologically and physically close. To ensure that this intimacy yields a positive relationship requires that a high level of attention to detail be paid to the climate created in organizations for people and for service, because this climate will determine the behavior of employees to customers–with all of the attendant customer satisfaction, loyalty, CLV and financial outcomes that follow.

It perhaps goes without saying but the fact is that it is difficult for companies to get all three legs of the stool functioning in alignment; if it was easy everyone would do it effectively. Because it is not easy, when a company gets it right there is the potential for competitive advantage precisely because it is not easy for others to duplicate. It may be easy to change price and it may be easy to change the product attributes but it is tough to get the offering, the marketing of it, and the delivery of it in alignment; achieving this alignment is not free but it seems to pay.

ON BECOMING A SERVICE EXCELLENCE ORGANIZATION

In the venues where we have discussed these concepts we are frequently asked questions about how to become a service quality organization. We have provided some information in various places in the paper on the issues and here summarize some of what we know about change. A lot has been written about organizational change (see Burke, 2003, for a recent take) and the difficulties of making it happen, but we offer here succinct answers to the more salient and frequently asked questions:

1. Can we become really service oriented without the commitment of top management? Yes. You only need top management to not get in the way. Top management has many stakeholders to which they must attend and sometimes they believe (sometimes with good reason!) that other stakeholders (politicians, for example) are more important than end-user consumers. Others lower in the organization, however, can take control of service quality and make it happen. For example, in a Human Resources department, selection, training, appraisal, and reward systems can consciously be built around service quality. First-line managers can also be trained to be more supportive, rewarding and reinforcing of service delivery excellence, and the people in operations and systems can be made sensitive to the needs of front-line service delivery workers for their support, too. Indeed, HR can play a leading role in creating a service climate (Schneider & White, 2004).

2. Is it more important to have a service climate, or to have a strong marketing campaign, or to have an excellent core product/service? Yes. These exist as a system and they are disaggregated at great peril in consumer service organizations. What the customers of a firm encounter is based on all of these: what it offers, how it markets itself, and the qualities of delivery. We have tried to teach organizations to never advertise "quality" because it has too many meanings and can raise expectations in strange and unpredictable ways–our motto is to advertise the core and deliver quality like Nordstrom does with its shoes.

3. Is the use of sophisticated information technology a positive, a negative, or a neutral in terms of service quality? Yes. If technology is introduced as a way to save expenses in delivery, we predict it will have a negative impact on an existing positive image. In addition, standardized information technology implemented in a standardized way denies all opportunities for distinctiveness, a key element of competitive advantage in the marketplace. Information technology implemented as part of a "learning organization" approach to improved service quality can pay important dividends in terms of creating a distinctive, reliable and memorable impression. By a "learning organization" we mean that the firm finds ways to capitalize on internal knowledge and competencies which, in the aggregate, make it superior to others. Capitalizing on such internal possibilities is an excellent use of information technology through the use, for example, of employee portals—gateways not only to capitalize on internal knowledge and competencies but to leverage external knowledge and competencies as well, in solving customer problems. The bottom line here is to answer the question: Why are we using this information technology? To cut costs or to enhance service quality? Citi has recently been advertising that if you call them you will get a real person; now that is competitive advantage.

4. How can we get our people to pay attention to service quality? With the active participation of service deliverers, develop tangible, specific, difficult goals for service quality improvement, establish the changes required to facilitate goal accomplishment, develop measurement systems for continuous evaluation of progress to the accomplishment of those goals, and share progress with all concerned (Latham, in press). There are two rules here: (1) Those who participate in the establishment of goals and the means of accomplishment turn out to be more committed to goal accomplishment, and (2) That which gets measured and rewarded gets attended to. Service quality does not happen as the result of coffee mugs, posters, or cash registers that flash a message ("say 'thank you'"); service quality happens when energies and competencies get focused on goal accomplishments that are measured and which have consequences.

5. If we want to become a service quality firm, where should we begin? Anywhere; just do it. Because organizations are systems, if you begin change in one location and follow your nose to the intended as well as unintended consequences of the change, you will know what to change next. In one insurance company we put in a new selection system for hiring telephone claims people and it then became clear that a new training program was required for these higher quality recruits—and then the supervisory selection process had to be changed to get better supervisors to work with these more talented, motivated, better-trained people. Another company began advertising its services to the public using existing employees and found that employees felt more identification with the firm due to the advertisements–and the number of excellent applicants for job openings jumped dramatically, again revealing the intimate connection between the internal and external worlds of organizations (Ployhart, Schneider & Schmitt, 2006).

6. *Who should be responsible for the change?* A line manager who is very well respected in the firm should have change responsibility for service quality/customer satisfaction (Schneider & Bowen, 1995). He or she should be given the same kinds of resources that the sales, operations, or finance departments have on which they can draw–including a special meeting with the CEO and his or her staff to report on plans and progress. The position needs to be established as a permanent position staffed with people with respected credentials or the program will be seen as just another attempt at change that will soon disappear.

Service excellence with all of its positive consequences is achieved only when the organization is conceptualized and managed with a single focus comprising its people, its core service, the delivery of same, and the marketing of same. The *involvement* of the maximum number of people in the service quality effort is the best way to ensure that such an effort will, indeed, have positive organizational consequences. When CLV and its obvious subcomponents (customer satisfaction, retention, and loyalty) is the strategic objective, management must ensure that they attend to all of the ways they send this message to people at all levels of the organization, and the degree to which the message is being played out in actuality must be carefully monitored. There is no better way to achieve a strategic goal than to create a climate for its achievement and then monitor the degree to which the policies, practices, and procedures are enacted, and the behaviors that must get supported, expected and rewarded are reaching the front line–where the customer meets the firm.

REFERENCES

Anderson, E. W., Fornell, C., & Mazvancheryl, S. K. (2004). Customer satisfaction and shareholder value. *Journal of Marketing, 68,* 172-185.

Barrick, M. R., & Mount, M. K. (1991). The Big Five personality dimensions and job performance: A meta-analysis. *Personnel Psychology, 44,* 1-26.

Bettencourt, L. A., & Brown, S. W. (1997). Customer-contact employees: Relationships among workplace fairness, job satisfaction and prosocial service behaviors. *Journal of Retailing, 73,* 39-61.

Bowen, J., & Ford, R. C. (2002). Managing service organizations: Does having a "thing" make a difference? *Journal of Management, 28,* 447-469.

Bowen, D. E., Gilliland, S., & Folger, R. (1999). HRM and service fairness: How being fair with employees spills over to customers. *Organizational Dynamics, 27*, 7-23.

Buckingham, M., & Coffman, C. (1999). *First, break all the rules: What the world's greatest managers do differently.* New York: Simon & Schuster.

Bund, B. E. (2006). *The outside-in corporation: How to build a customer-centric organization for breakthrough results.* New York: McGraw-Hill.

Burke, W. W. (2003). *Organization change: Theory and practice.* Thousand Oaks, CA: Sage.

Dean, A. M. (2004). Links between organisational and customer variables in service delivery: Evidence, contradictions, and challenges. *International Journal of Service Industry Management, 15*, 332-350.

Frei, R. L., & McDaniel, M. A. (1998). Validity of customer service measures on personnel selection: A review of criterion and construct evidence. *Human Performance, 11*, 1-27.

Grönroos, C. (1990). *Service management and marketing: Managing the moments of truth in service competition.* Lexington, MA: Lexington Books.

Gruca, T. S., & Rego, L. L. (2005). Customer satisfaction, cash flow, and shareholder value. *Journal of Marketing, 69*, 115-130.

Heskett, J. L., Sasser, W. E., Jr., & Schlesinger, L. A. (1997). *The service profit chain.* New York: Free Press.

Hogan, R. (1996). A socio-analytic view of the Five-Factor Model. In J. S. Wiggins (Ed.), *The Five-Factor Model in personality: Theoretical perspectives.* New York: Guilford.

Hogan, R. (2004). Personality psychology for researchers. In B. Schneider & D. B. Smith (Eds.), *Personality and organizations* (pp. 3-23). Mahwah, NJ: Erlbaum.

Hogan, J., Hogan, R., & Busch, C. M. (1984). How to measure service orientation. *Journal of Applied Psychology, 69*, 3-11.

James, L. R., James, L. A., & Ashe, D. K. (1990). The meaning of organizations: The role of cognition and values. In B. Schneider (Ed.), *Organizational climate and culture* (pp. 40-84). San Francisco: Jossey-Bass.

Latham, G. P. (In Press). *Work Motivation: History, theory, research, and practice.* Thousand Oaks, CA: Sage.

Lewin, K. (1935). *A dynamic theory of personality.* New York: McGraw-Hill.

Lewin, K., Lippitt, R., & White, R. K. (1939). Patterns of aggressive behavior in experimentally created "social climates." *Journal of Social Psychology, 10*, 271-299.

Lovelock, C., & Wirtz, J. (2004). *Services marketing: People, technology, strategy, 5th ed.* Upper Saddle River, NJ: Pearson/Prentice-Hall.

Lytle, R. S., Hom, P. W., & Mokwa, M. P. (1998). SERV*OR: A managerial measure of service orientation. *Journal of Retailing, 74*, 455-489.

Macey, W. H., & Schneider, B. (In Press). Employee experiences and customer satisfaction: Toward a framework for survey design with a focus on service climate. In A. I. Kraut (Ed.), *Getting action from organizational surveys: New concepts, technologies and applications.* New York: Pfeiffer/Wiley.

Martin, J. (2002). *Organizational culture: Mapping the terrain.* Thousand Oaks, CA: Sage.

Michaels, R. E., & Day, R. L. (1985). Measuring customer orientation of sales people: A replication with industrial buyers. *Journal of Marketing Research, 22,* 443-446.

Morgan, R. M. (2000). Relationship marketing and marketing strategy: The evolution of relationship marketing strategy within the organization. In J. N. Sheth & A. Parvatiyar (Eds.), *Handbook of relationship marketing* (pp. 481-504). Thousand Oaks, CA: Sage.

Ployhart, R. E., Schneider, B., & Schmitt, N. (2006). *Staffing organizations: Contemporary practice and theory, 3rd ed.* Mahwah, NJ: Erlbaum.

Reichheld, F. F. (1996). *The loyalty effect.* Boston: Harvard Business School Press.

Reynoso, J., & Moores, B. (1995). Towards the measurement of internal service quality. *International Journal of Service Industry Management, 6,* 64-83.

Ryan, A. M., & Ployhart, R. E. (2003). Customer service behavior. In R. J. Klimoski, W. C. Borman, & D. R. Ilgen (Eds.), *Handbook of Psychology (Vol. 12)* (pp. 377-397). Hoboken, NJ: Wiley & Sons.

Salanova, M., Agut, S. & Peiró, J. M. (2005). Linking organizational resources and work engagement to employee performance and customer loyalty: The mediation of service climate. *Journal of Applied Psychology, 90,* 1217-1227.

Schein, E. H. (2000). Sense and nonsense about culture and climate. In N. M. Ashkanasy, C. Wilderom, & M. F. Peterson (Eds.), *Handbook of organizational culture and climate* (pp. xxiii-xxx). Thousand Oaks, CA: Sage.

Schneider, B. (1975). Organizational climates: An essay. *Personnel Psychology, 28,* 447-479.

Schneider, B. (1987). The people make the place. *Personnel Psychology, 40,* 437-453.

Schneider, B. (2000). The psychological life of organizations. In N. M. Ashkanasy, C. Wilderom, & M. F. Peterson (Eds.), *Handbook of organizational culture and climate* (pp. xvii-xxi). Thousand Oaks, CA: Sage.

Schneider, B., Ashworth, S. D., Higgs, A. C., & Carr, L. (1996). Design, validity and use of strategically focused employee attitude surveys. *Personnel Psychology, 49,* 695-705.

Schneider, B., & Bowen, D. E. (1985), Employee and customer perceptions of service in banks: Replication and extension. *Journal of Applied Psychology, 70,* 423-433.

Schneider, B., & Bowen, D. E. (1995). *Winning the service game.* Boston, MA: Harvard Business School Press.

Schneider, B., Ehrhart, M. W., Mayer, D. E., Saltz, J., & Niles-Jolly, K. A. (2005). Understanding organizational-customer linkages in service organizations. *Academy of Management Journal, 48,* 1017-1032.

Schneider, B., Macey, W. H., Young, S., & Lee, W. (2006). *Organizational drivers of the American Customer Satisfaction Index (ACSI).* Working paper. Rolling Meadows, IL: Valtera Corporation.

Schneider, B., Wheeler, J. K., & Cox, J. F. (1992). A passion for service: Using content analysis to explicate service climate themes. *Journal of Applied Psychology, 77,* 705-716.

Schneider, B., & White, S. S. (2004). *Service quality: Research perspectives.* Thousand Oaks, CA: Sage.

Schneider, B., White, S. S., & Paul, M. C. (1998). Linking service climate and customer perceptions of service quality: Test of a causal model. *Journal of Applied Psychology, 83,* 150-163.

Sheth, J. N., & Parvatiyar, A. (1995). Relationship marketing in consumer markets: Antecedents and consequences. *Journal of the Academy of Marketing Science, 23,* 255-271.

Tax, S. S., & Brown, S. W. (2000). Service recovery: Research insights and practice. In T. A. Swartz & D. Iacobucci (Eds.), *Handbook of services marketing and management* (pp. 271-286). Thousand Oaks, CA: Sage.

Tobin, J. (1969). A general equilibrium approach to monetary theory. *Journal of Money, Credit, and Banking, 1,* 15-29.

Weick, K. E. (1995). *Sensemaking in organizations.* Thousand Oaks, CA: Sage.

Wiley, J. W. (1996). Linking survey results to customer satisfaction and business performance. In A. I. Kraut (Ed.), *Organizational surveys: Tools for assessment and change* (pp. 330-359). San Francisco: Jossey-Bass.

Zahorik, A. J., & Rust, R. T. (1992), Modeling the impact of service quality on profitability: A review. In T. A. Swartz, D. E. Bowen, & S. W. Brown (Eds.), *Advances in services marketing and management* (pp. 247-276). Greenwich, CT: JAI.

Zohar, D. (2000). A group-level model of safety climate: Testing the effect of group climate on microaccidents in manufacturing jobs. *Journal of Applied Psychology, 85,* 587-596.

doi:10.1300/J366v05n02_07

The Future of Managing Customers as Assets

Timothy L. Keiningham

Ipsos Loyalty

Lerzan Aksoy

Koc University, Istanbul, Turkey

David Bejou

Virginia State University

SUMMARY. Most companies do a very poor job of determining the economic value of their customers. There are three primary reasons that this has been the case: (1) inadequacy of technology, (2) managements' internal focus on products (as opposed to customers), and (3) inadequacy of accounting systems. Each of these areas, however, has undergone rapid transformation in terms of their sophistication and

Timothy L. Keiningham, MBA, is Senior Vice President and Head of Consulting, Ipsos Loyalty, Morris Corporation Center 2, 1 Upper Pond Road, Building D, Parsippany, NJ 07054 (E-mail: tim.keiningham@ipsos-na.com).

Lerzan Aksoy, PhD, is Assistant Professor of Marketing, Koc University, College of Administrative Sciences and Economics, Rumeli Feneri Yolu, Sariyer 80910 Istanbul, Turkey (E-mail: laksoy@ku.edu.tr).

David Bejou, PhD, is Dean, School of Business, Virginia State University, P.O. Box 9398, Petersburg, VA 23806 (E-mail: dbejou@vsu.edu).

[Haworth co-indexing entry note]: "The Future of Managing Customers as Assets." Keiningham, Timothy L., Lerzan Aksoy, and David Bejou. Co-published simultaneously in *Journal of Relationship Marketing* (Best Business Books, an imprint of The Haworth Press, Inc.) Vol. 5, No. 2/3, 2006, pp. 133-138; and: *Customer Lifetime Value: Reshaping the Way We Manage to Maximize Profits* (ed: David Bejou, Timothy L. Keiningham, and Lerzan Aksoy) Best Business Books, an imprint of The Haworth Press, Inc., 2006, pp. 133-138. Single or multiple copies of this article are available for a fee from The Haworth Document Delivery Service [1-800-HAWORTH, 9:00 a.m. - 5:00 p.m. (EST). E-mail address: docdelivery@haworthpress.com].

managerial usefulness. As a result, it is manifest destiny that asset valuation and management will evolve to the evaluation of a company's most fundamental asset, its customers (i.e., customer lifetime value). Most managers have come to accept this inevitability. What managers fail to realize is just how radically an understanding of customer lifetime value will transform the business landscape. It will dramatically impact the breadth and type of data collected; the way managers view and segment customers; the types of experiences firms offer customers; the metrics executives provide to the financial markets; and the way companies structure and staff their organizations. doi:10.1300/J366v05n02_08 *[Article copies available for a fee from The Haworth Document Delivery Service: 1-800-HAWORTH. E-mail address: <docdelivery@haworthpress.com> Website: <http://www.HaworthPress.com> © 2006 by The Haworth Press, Inc. All rights reserved.]*

KEYWORDS. Customer lifetime value, strategic management, valuation, market value

As more and more managers rightfully treat their customers as the preeminent assets that they are for their firms, the need to understand customer profitability will naturally become paramount. "Assets" are managed based on their value to the firm. No reasonable manager would consider managing his operations without an understanding of the value of plant, equipment, or inventory; in fact, managers even assign a value to goodwill.

When it comes to customers, however, most companies do a very poor job of determining their value. In the opinion of the authors, there are three primary reasons for this: (1) inadequacy of then-current technology, (2) managements' internal focus on products (as opposed to customers), and (3) inadequacy of then-current accounting systems.

INADEQUACY OF TECHNOLOGY

The ability to collect and manage the data necessary to determine individual customer profitability is a product of the current stage of the information age. Measuring and managing customer lifetime value is data-driven and data-intensive. Only very recently have systems and software become cost-effective for collecting and manipulating the requisite customer data.

As a result, corporate spending on CRM (customer relationship management) systems has skyrocketed. As a testament to that growth, IDC reports that the CRM applications market was \$8.8 billion in 2004, a gain of eight percent over 2003 (*Customer Relationship Management,* 2005). In fact, it is not unheard of now for firms to collect terabytes of data on their customers' behaviors (Kaczmarski, Jiang, & Pease, 2003).

MANAGEMENTS' INTERNAL FOCUS ON PRODUCTS

The second reason is based on the management legacy of the prior century. As noted in the introduction, efficient operations were the primary driver of business empires of the past. As these initial production-driven empires developed, the understanding of their own actual cost of operations was often shrouded in mystery. For example, Ford Motor Company (under the leadership of Henry Ford) had no real idea as to the cost of its operations. In his book, *The Reckoning*, Halberstam (1986, pp. 99-100) describes Arjay Miller's rude awaking upon joining the firm in 1946 when he sought a profit forecast for the next month (Miller later became president of Ford),

> *Miller went down to the office building, where the financial operations were kept . . . there he found thousands of bills, and they were dividing them into categories, A, B, C, D. The piles were immense, some several feet high. To Miller's amazement, the bookkeepers were actually estimating how many million dollars there were per foot of paper. . . . Twenty years earlier it had been worse . . . [Bills were] broken down into two categories, those under \$10 an item and those over. Serious investigation had shown that the average figure for bills under \$10 was \$2.43, and so they used that figure to multiply against the gross weight of the paper.*

The ability to understand, and thereby drive down, the cost of operations became an ever-increasing source of competitive advantage. Alfred Sloan, the legendary CEO of General Motors, used this knowledge to transform modern management. By finding ways to minimize the cost associated with variety, General Motors was able to offer multiple makes and models of automobiles without increasing production costs (Raff, 1991).

The quest for a better understanding of the value of operational assets evolved over time. For example, the manufacturing quality movement showed that the "cost of quality" had been consistently understated

(Deming, 1988; Juran, 1964). Additionally, activity-based cost accounting developed to provide a clearer picture of the value of various tangible assets throughout the manufacturing process (Ochs & Bicheno, 1991).

EVOLUTION OF ACCOUNTING MEASURES

The finance literature is replete with "better," more granular methods of valuing tangible assets. Despite improved methods, however, researchers and managers have questioned the ability of professional analysts to effectively predict the financial performance of firms (for example, see Fama, 1970 & 1991; Malkiel, 1973; Schwed, 1940).

Recently, marketers have proposed that much of the problem with predicting firm performance is that the models used lack non-financial, customer-based metrics (Hogan et al., 2002; Gupta, Lehmann, & Stuart, 2004). Traditional accounting focuses on measuring tangible data reported in a firm's financial statements. Advocates of non-financial metrics argue that intangible assets such as customer equity are critical elements of firm value (Amir & Lev, 1996; Srivastava, Shervani, & Fahey, 1998). According to Gupta and Lehmann (2003, p. 10), "This interest in intangibles arises from the recognition that [the] market value of the largest 500 corporations in the United States is almost six times the book value (the net value of physical and financial assets as stated on the balance sheet). In other words, of every six dollars in the market value of the firm, only one dollar is represented in the balance sheet."

MANIFEST DESTINY

Therefore, because of the combination of these three forces, it is manifest destiny that asset valuation and management will evolve to the evaluation of a company's most fundamental asset: its customers. In fact, the call for understanding customer lifetime value (CLV) is beginning to reach fever pitch in management journals, and become the crusade of managers throughout the world.

Most managers accept the inevitability of CLV measurement and management (although they may argue as to when this is likely to occur). What managers fail to realize, however, is just how radically it will transform the business landscape. It will dramatically impact the breadth and type of data we collect; the way we view and segment, and the types of experiences we offer customers; the metrics we provide to the financial markets; and the way we structure and staff our companies.

Whether or not CLV represents the Holy Grail of competitive weapons is open to debate . . . history will be the ultimate judge. But one thing is certain: CLV provides clear goal posts for maximizing profitability. Those firms that are able to understand and manage CLV first will have a clear advantage over their competitors. They will be able to evaluate the myriad business decisions they must make based upon the return on investment. As a result, they can manage their scarce resources and direct their spending where it counts most: to enhance the value of their most precious assets–their customers.

REFERENCES

Amir, E. & Lev, B. (1996). Value-relevance of nonfinancial information: The wireless communication industry. *Journal of Accounting and Economics, 22,* 1-3 (August-December), 3-30.

Anonymous (2005). Destination CRM dashboard: The CRM industry is here to play. *Customer Relationship Management, 9,* 10 (October), 18.

Deming, W. E. (1988). *Out of the crisis.* Cambridge, MA: Massachusetts Institute of Technology.

Fama, E. (1970). Efficient capital markets: A review of theory and empirical work. *Journal of Finance, 25* (2), 383-417.

Fama, E. (1991). Efficient capital markets: A review of theory and empirical work. *Journal of Finance, 46,* 5 (December), 1575-1617.

Gupta, S. & Lehmann, D. R. (2003). Customers as assets. *Journal of Interactive Marketing, 17* (1), 9-24.

Gupta, S., Lehmann, D. R. & Stuart, J. A. (2004). Valuing customers. *Journal of Marketing Research, 41,* 1 (February), 7-18.

Halberstam, D. (1986). *The reckoning* (paperback). New York, NY: William Morrow & Co.

Hogan, J. E., Lehmann, D. E., Merino, M., Srivastava, R. K., Thomas, J. S. & Verhoef, P. C. (2002). Linking customer assets to financial performance. *Journal of Service Research, 5,* 1 (August), 26-38.

Juran, J. M. (1964). *Managerial breakthrough.* New York: McGraw-Hill Book Co.

Kaczmarski, M., Jiang, T. & Pease, D. A. (2003). Beyond backup toward storage management. *IBM Systems Journal, 42* (2), 322-337.

Malkiel, B. (1973). *A random walk down Wall Street.* New York: W.W. Norton & Company.

Ochs, R. & Bicheno, J. (1991). Activity-based cost management linked to manufacturing strategy. *Industrial Management, 33,* 1 (Jan/Feb), 11-16.

Raff, D. M. G. (1991). Making cars and making money in the interwar automobile industry: Economies of scale and scope and the manufacturing behind the marketing. *Business History Review, 65*, 4 (Winter), 721-753.

Schwed, F., Jr. (1940). *Where are the customers' yachts? Or, a good hard look at Wall Street.* New York: Simon and Schuster.

Srivastava, R. K., Shervani, T. A. & Fahey, L. (1998). Market-based assets and shareholder value: A framework for analysis. *Journal of Marketing, 62*, 2-18.

doi:10.1300/J366v05n02_08

Index

Page numbers followed by an *f* or *t* indicate figures and tables.

BOOK ORDER FORM!

Order a copy of this book with this form or online at:
http://www.HaworthPress.com/store/product.asp?sku= 5950

Customer Lifetime Value
Reshaping the Way We Manage to Maximize Profits

—— in softbound at $18.00 ISBN-13: 978-0-7890-3436-6 / ISBN-10: 0-7890-3436-0.
—— in hardbound at $36.00 ISBN-13: 978-0-7890-3435-9 / ISBN-10: 0-7890-3435-2.

COST OF BOOKS _____

POSTAGE & HANDLING _____
US: $4.00 for first book & $1.50
for each additional book
Outside US: $5.00 for first book
& $2.00 for each additional book.

SUBTOTAL _____

In Canada: add 6% GST. _____

STATE TAX _____
CA, IL, IN, MN, NJ, NY, OH, PA & SD residents
please add appropriate local sales tax.

FINAL TOTAL _____
If paying in Canadian funds, convert
using the current exchange rate,
UNESCO coupons welcome.

❑ **BILL ME LATER:**
Bill-me option is good on US/Canada/
Mexico orders only; not good to jobbers,
wholesalers, or subscription agencies.

❑ **Signature** _____

❑ **Payment Enclosed: $**_____

❑ **PLEASE CHARGE TO MY CREDIT CARD:**
❑ Visa ❑ MasterCard ❑ AmEx ❑ Discover
❑ Diner's Club ❑ Eurocard ❑ JCB

Account #_____

Exp Date_____

Signature_____
(Prices in US dollars and subject to change without notice.)

PLEASE PRINT ALL INFORMATION OR ATTACH YOUR BUSINESS CARD

Name

Address

City   State/Province   Zip/Postal Code

Country

Tel   Fax

E-Mail

May we use your e-mail address for confirmations and other types of information? ❑Yes ❑No We appreciate receiving
your e-mail address. Haworth would like to e-mail special discount offers to you, as a preferred customer.
We will never share, rent, or exchange your e-mail address. We regard such actions as an invasion of your privacy.

Order from your **local bookstore** or directly from
The Haworth Press, Inc. 10 Alice Street, Binghamton, New York 13904-1580 • USA
Call our toll-free number (1-800-429-6784) / Outside US/Canada: (607) 722-5857
Fax: 1-800-895-0582 / Outside US/Canada: (607) 771-0012
E-mail your order to us: orders@HaworthPress.com

For orders outside US and Canada, you may wish to order through your local
sales representative, distributor, or bookseller.
For information, see http://HaworthPress.com/distributors

(Discounts are available for individual orders in US and Canada only, not booksellers/distributors.)

Please photocopy this form for your personal use.
www.HaworthPress.com

BOF06